WALT DISNEY'S

BAMBI

THE STORY AND THE FILM

BY OLLIE JOHNSTON AND FRANK THOMAS

STEWART, TABORI & CHANG
NEW YORK

We dedicate this book to
WALT DISNEY
who asked for it fifty years ago.

I'd like to see a book—an edition of Bambi—put out afterwards, and I'd just like to see the text all broken up with these sketches.

WALT DISNEY, *Story meeting notes, December 12, 1939*

Sorry, Walt—you always said we were slow.

Published in 1990 by
Stewart, Tabori & Chang, Inc.
575 Broadway, New York, New York 10012

Library of Congress Cataloging-in-Publication Data

Johnston, Ollie, 1912-
    Walt Disney's Bambi: the story and the film/by Ollie Johnston and Frank Thomas.
        p.   cm.
    Summary: Text and artwork from the animated film "Bambi" unfold the story of the deer who grows up to be King of the Forest and reveal the creative struggles and victories behind the making of the movie.
    ISBN 1-55670-160-8
    [1. Bambi (Motion picture)]   I. Thomas, Frank, 1912-   II. Walt Disney Company.   III. Title.   IV. Title: Bambi.
PN1997.B24335J64   1990   90-34497
791.43′72—dc20

Distributed in the U.S. by Workman Publishing,
708 Broadway, New York, New York 10003
Distributed in Canada by Canadian Manda Group,
P.O. Box 920 Station U, Toronto, Ontario M8Z 5P9
Distributed in all other territories by
Little, Brown and Company, International Division,
34 Beacon Street, Boston, Massachusetts 02108

Printed in Japan

10 9 8 7 6 5 4 3 2 1

CONTENTS

PREFACE

Of all the endearing films that Walt Disney created with his staff, none has had as strong an impact on viewers as *Bambi*. It has a beauty of thought and visualization, an integrity, a fantasy, and a power that lives with people the rest of their lives.

The book by Felix Salten was an outstanding literary work that combined philosophy, poetry, and rich imagination, but there was no story structure suitable for an animated cartoon. From the romance of the North Wind and the gentler wind from the south to the intimate thoughts shared by the last two leaves on a tree to Bambi's final realization that man is not all-powerful, every chapter was built on inner feelings and realistic action.

In 1936, could the crude new art form known as animation portray such subtle ideas? The answer was no. Yet Walt and a key portion of his staff believed in the project and spent seven years constantly searching for ways to transfer the concepts beautifully expressed in words to an equally appealing visual form.

Walt first suggested this book in 1939 when his hopes for *Bambi* were becoming realities and confidence was building excitement for the outstanding film we were creating. There was little warning at that time of the cataclysmic events that would, over the next two years, bring the Disney Studio to the brink of closing forever. Bleak survival allowed neither time nor talent to put out the beautiful book that had been envisioned.

Forty years later while we were doing research for our first book, *Disney Animation: The Illusion of Life,* the treasures destined for Walt's *Bambi* book were rediscovered. In addition to outstanding artwork, there was an almost complete set of story meeting notes, including Walt's comments, which revealed the tortured and turbulent history of the whole production process, year by year. We have quoted these exchanges faithfully.

Dialogue under consideration for the animated characters was always written in capital letters to avoid confusion with the comments in the general discussion and has been reproduced the same way here. We par-ticipated in many of these meetings ourselves and still remember the emotions, the laughter, the concern, the moments of quiet followed by noisy confusion, the disagreements, all things that the transcripts fail to capture. Yet they do reveal the problems, the attempted solutions, and Walt's unique way of creating his classic films.

This book is divided into three parts: first, the story we told on the screen, with the humor and warmth and pathos that has made this film such an important part of our culture. The illustrations are the same drawings—from story sketches to layouts to animation—which solved the storytelling problems that haunted us throughout production.

The second part of this book is about making the picture, starting with the first meetings initiated by Sidney Franklin, the top MGM producer-director who had hoped to make a live action film of the book. He gradually realized that if it could be done at all, it would be only through the magic of animation. *Bambi* was not a type of picture anyone had ever made before and it proved to be extremely elusive.

Finally, in the third part we have created a compendium of the animation drawings that pinned down the picture's elusiveness and gave life to the wonderful characters that Walt had dreamed of. These drawings express the acting and the personality that is the magic of *Bambi*.

The magnificence of the completed film impressed Sidney Franklin greatly and he told Walt, "It was so far beyond what I expected. . . . I think it is really beautiful and one of your best pictures."

This book should have been published years ago, but fortunately can be done at this time while much of the artwork still exists and many of the fine artists are around to add their stories and memories to our own. Viewing the film today we are no longer aware of the difficulties, the calamities, the emotional struggles. We easily slip into the simplicity and beauty of the imaginary forest that is so real and meet again the delightful creatures who will live there forever.

ACKNOWLEDGMENTS

Putting this book together has been a very complicated adventure. No single person knew the whole story of the making of the *Bambi* film completed a half-century ago. Much has been forgotten, memories are tainted by emotional events of the past, and there are conflicting stories on everything, even down to which artist was responsible for which painting. But assistance came to us quickly from many quarters and we give our special thanks to the following:

To Wayne Morris and Wendall Mohler of Publications for giving the Studio's permission to do the Bambi book back in 1986; to Esther Ewert, Director of the Disney Art Program, who fell in love with the book when it was placed in her hands upon Wayne's retirement, and to the unflappable Dave Cleghorn, who was put in charge of the project;

To publisher Andy Stewart for recognizing the beauty and worth of the drawings and paintings that had been considered as only "cartoon art" for so many years; to J.C. Suarès and Paul Zakris, who created dramatic pages for exciting drawings; and to our editor, Ann Campbell, who had the perplexing job of sorting out the words of artists more used to expressing their ideas in visual terms;

To Dave Smith, head of Archives, and his wonderful staff, Paula Sigman-Lowery, Rose Motzko, Karen Brower, and Jennie Hendrickson, who searched out hidden drawings, story meeting notes, private correspondence, and even made a home away from home for us in their crowded office space;

To the now-retired Leroy Anderson, former head of the Animation Research Library and to Kay Salz, the new department head, who gave so much assistance with the material stored away in their collection of drawings, layouts, and backgrounds from the film; to Kevin Fagan's Drabble strip for mentioning Bambi;

To Joanne Warren and Janice Loveton in the Photo Library, who were so supportive in helping us obtain pictures of the personnel and their work;

To Howard Green, Director of Studio Communications, who has been instrumental in keeping our Bambi book alive in the media;

To Martha Armstrong Hand, widow of Dave Hand, for allowing us to quote from his book of memoirs which she published posthumously, and for offering us a special collection of the atmosphere sketches he had saved;

To Stan Spohn for sharing the four paintings by Harold Miles that he had saved, and to Helen and Robert McIntosh for letting us use paintings by Ty Wong, Maurice Noble, and others from their personal collection;

To Mike Barrier, whose personal files furnished us with interviews that existed nowhere else;

To the men and women of the Bambi unit, who many years ago contributed such magnificent work to the picture. It has been a thrill to once again handle this superb collection without which there would be neither book nor film.

And finally, our special thanks to the Disney Studio employees, past and present, who graciously shared their time; their skills; their stories, impressions, and memories; and even their treasured drawings. We owe these people a great debt of gratitude:

Ed Aardal, Hal Ambro, Jack Atwood, Bob Bamford, Roy Brewer, Elsa Timmner Codrick, Chuck Couch, Marc Davis, Jules Engel, Carl Fallberg, Catherine Faulkner, Joe Grant, Larry Ishino, Travis Johnson, Bob Jones, Bill Justice, Lew Keller, Eva Jane Sinclair Kinney, Jack Kinney, Larry Lansburgh, Eric Larson, Bob McCrea, Maurice Noble, Ken O'Brien, Steve Rogers, Paul Satterfield, Louie Schmitt, Mel Shaw, Grace Simpson, Charles Solomon, Stacy St. Pierre, McLaren Stewart, Robyn Tynan, Clair Weeks, Retta Scott Worcester, Tyrus Wong, and Bob Youngquist.

THE STORY

THE NEW PRINCE

In the depths of the forest, dawn was breaking. Trees grew so thickly here that the morning's first rays of light could hardly break through. The air was still and blue with mist. The faint, silvery sound of a distant waterfall and the breeze rustling the new spring leaves were the only noises to be heard.

A few drowsy birds were just beginning to greet the day as a huge old owl swooped silently toward the hollow tree where he made his home. The world was waking up all around him. A bright-eyed wood mouse slipped out of her nest to wash her face in a dewdrop. Three baby sparrows cheeped shrilly as their father brought them their first meal of the day—a cluster of berries. And with every second, the pale sunbeams grew brighter.

The young rabbit Thumper, who was always the first of his family to arise, was waking up slowly, yawning and scratching as he did every morning.

But the owl was ready for bed. He had been hunting all night, and he was tired. With a sigh

The sound of a waterfall in the distance could be heard *(right, top);* While baby birds cheeped over their breakfast *(middle),* the owl prepared for bed *(right),* and a wood mouse washed her face in a dewdrop *(below).* Opposite: The new prince. Overleaf: Early dawn in the forest.

13

"It's happened! The new prince is here!" *(top);* From every corner, animals popped out of their hiding places and raced to the thicket *(above and below)*.

he alighted on a branch, waddled into his hole, and fluffed up his feathers. His drowsy eyes dipped shut, and he fell asleep.

He didn't get to stay asleep very long.

"He's here! He's here! He's here!" called an excited voice.

A bluebird darted through the air to perch on the tree next to the owl's. "He's here! Follow me!" she twittered, and flew off.

From every corner animals popped out of their hiding places and raced after her. Mrs. Quail streaked swiftly along the forest floor, her babies trailing after her as if they were on a string.

Thumper's sisters burst out of their house, tumbling over each other and their brother in their anxiety to get to the thicket first.

Thumper dashed to the foot of the owl's tree and began drumming frantically on the ground with his right foot.

"Wake up! Wake up!" he hollered at the top of his lungs.

The owl shook himself irritably and squinted down at Thumper. "Oh, what now?" he groaned.

"Wake *up*, Friend Owl!" the little rabbit persisted.

"Why? What's going on around here, anyway? Can't a person get some—"

"It's happened! The new prince is born!" shouted Thumper. "We're going to see him! Come on, you'd better hurry up!" And he dashed into the underbrush after his sisters.

"The new prince!" The owl gave his feathers a hasty preening and soared into the air.

The prince was a tiny fawn, only two hours old. When the animals reached the thicket where he had been born, he was curled up, sound asleep, next to his mother's warm side. He didn't even stir as the creatures of the forest gathered into a circle around him.

"Oh, my!" said Mrs. Raccoon with a wistful sigh. "Isn't he just the most—"

"Oh, my! Beautiful!" echoed hushed maternal voices from all around the circle.

"Yes, indeed," said the owl from a bough overhead. "This is—ahem—quite an occasion. Yes, sir. It isn't every day a prince is born." He bent low in a courtly bow to the fawn's mother. "You are to be congratulated."

"Thank you," said the prince's mother quietly. She leaned over and gave her baby a loving nudge. "Wake up," she whispered. "Come on, dear. We have company."

"This is—ahem—quite an occasion. You are to be congratulated," said the owl *(below);* "Thank you," said the prince's mother *(bottom).*

Slowly, slowly the tiny fawn's head lifted. He stared wonderingly at the creatures standing in front of him.

"Hello, Prince!" squeaked a mouse timidly.

At once a chorus of greetings sprang up, and the owl let out a loud "hoo-hoo"—so loud that the fawn turned away and burrowed his face into his mother's side. Then he gathered up his courage and peeked out again. And this time he managed a shy smile.

"Look!" called Thumper excitedly. "He's trying to get up!"

He was—but it wasn't working very well. Try as he might, the fawn couldn't get his slender legs to work together.

"He's kinda wobbly, isn't he?" noted Thumper.

"*Thumper!*" gasped Mrs. Rabbit. She gave a flustered smile at the fawn's mother.

Thumper scowled. "Well, he is," he muttered, kicking at the ground in embarrassment. "Aren't you?" he asked the fawn.

The fawn nodded eagerly. He hadn't understood a word.

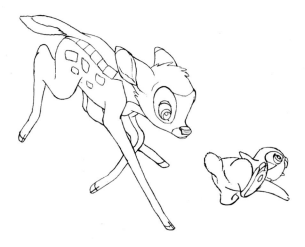

Slowly the fawn's head lifted *(top);* "Look! He's trying to get up!" *(middle);* "He's kinda wobbly, isn't he?" noted Thumper *(bottom and right).*

The owl chuckled. "Looks to me like he's getting kind of sleepy," he said. "I think it's time we all left."

There was a murmur of protest from the younger animals. But the owl leaned over and fixed such a schoolmasterish glare on the crowd that they began to melt into the woods without another word.

Only Thumper still lingered in the thicket. "Whatcha gonna call him?" he asked the fawn's mother when everyone else had left.

She smiled at him. "Well, I think I'll call him Bambi," she answered.

Thumper frowned thoughtfully, as if the choice were up to him. "Bambi," he repeated, trying it out. "*Bambi.* Yup, I guess that'll do, all right." And he hopped off to find his family.

Bambi's mother glanced down at her baby, who was sound asleep again.

"Bambi," she murmured tenderly. "My little Bambi."

As the mother and child settled down together, high on the hill above the thicket the Great Prince of the Forest kept watch.

"Oh, my! Beautiful," echoed the visitors *(top);* "Psst—I think it's time we all left." *(middle);* The Great Prince of the Forest watched over his family *(bottom).*

THE FOREST

Walking already, well, what do you know?" commented the gray squirrel as Bambi and his mother strolled through the forest. Bambi was three days old now. As far as *he* was concerned, he was the best walker the forest had ever seen, though sometimes his legs did get tangled. And he was proud that so many of the forest creatures had gotten the chance to see him.

He had met Mrs. Quail and her babies scurrying through the underbrush as though they were late for an appointment. He had met Mrs. Possum and her babies, all hanging jauntily upside down from a tree branch. He had met Mr. Mole, who had popped up right under Bambi's nose. "Good mornin'," Mr. Mole had said politely. "Nice, sunny day." He had squinted up at the bright sky, winced a little, and returned with relief to his tunneling. The curious little fawn tried to follow the mole's path, but wound up tumbling over some reeds as his mother and the rabbit family looked on.

"He doesn't walk very well, does he?" asked Thumper with interest.

"*Thumper!*" scolded his mother. "*What* did your father tell you this morning?"

Thumper sighed. "'If you can't say somethin' nice, don't say nothin' at all,'" he muttered, frowning down at the ground.

Bambi and his mother strolled through the forest *(top);* He had met Mrs. Quail and her babies *(middle)* and Mrs. Possum and her babies—all hanging upside down! *(bottom);* "Nice sunny day," said Mr. Mole *(left).* OPPOSITE: Bambi was proud to meet so many of his neighbors.

"Thumper, what did your father tell you?"
"If you can't say somethin' nice, don't say
nothin' at all."

Bambi's mother leaned over and nuzzled Bambi's shoulder a little. "Come on, Bambi," she urged gently. "Get up. Try again."

"Come on! Come on!" squealed Thumper and his sisters excitedly. "Get up! Get up! You can do it!"

And—after he'd managed to sort his legs out—Bambi pranced happily off after his new friends.

But, trying to follow the little rabbits, the young deer had difficulties with a large log lying across the path.

"C'mon, you can do it," encouraged Thumper. "Hop over it. Like this." All the bunnies chimed in as they leapt back and forth over the log, "Hop over it! Hop over it!"

Bambi stepped back to gather momentum, but his hop landed him smack-dab on top of the log.

"You didn't hop far enough," said Thumper wisely.

Bambi finally got all of himself over the log, but in the process his legs became tangled once more, causing the bunnies all to scatter— just in case he might fall on them.

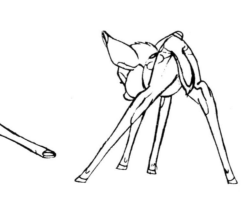

As far as Bambi was concerned, he was the best walker the forest had ever seen *(above)*. OPPOSITE: Bambi pranced off happily after his new friends *(top);* "You didn't hop far enough." *(middle);* "Get up! Get up! You can do it!" *(bottom and below).* OVERLEAF: Bambi was three days old.

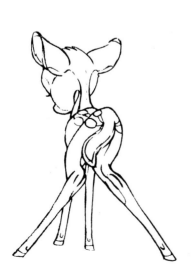

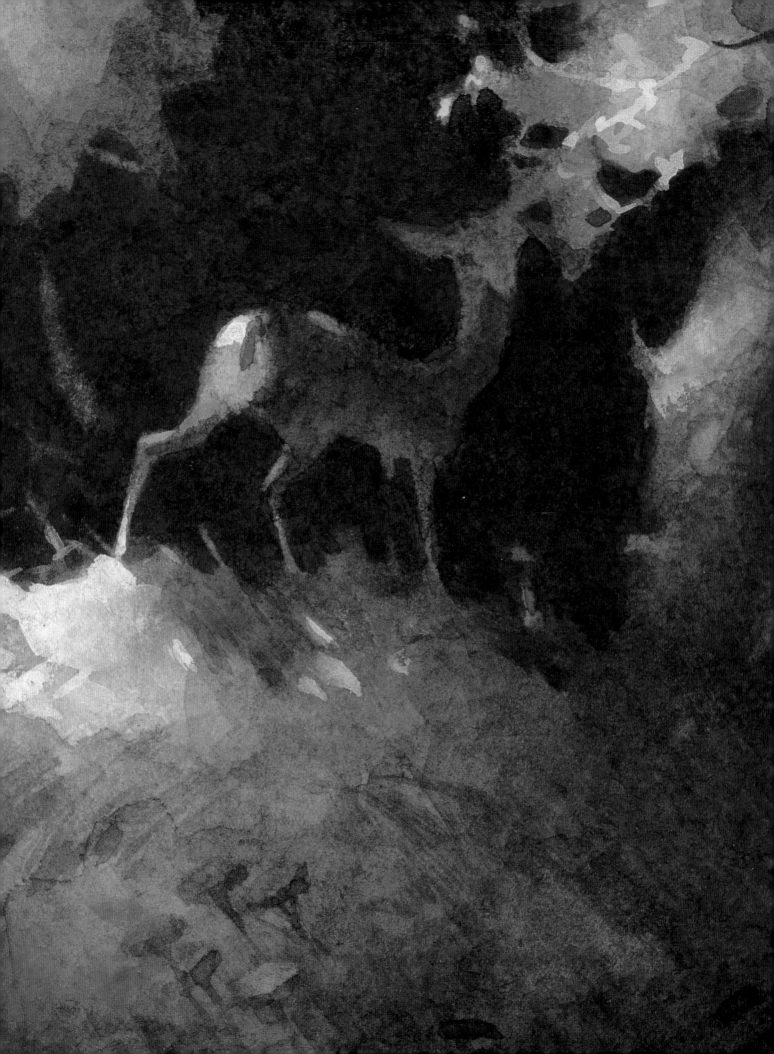

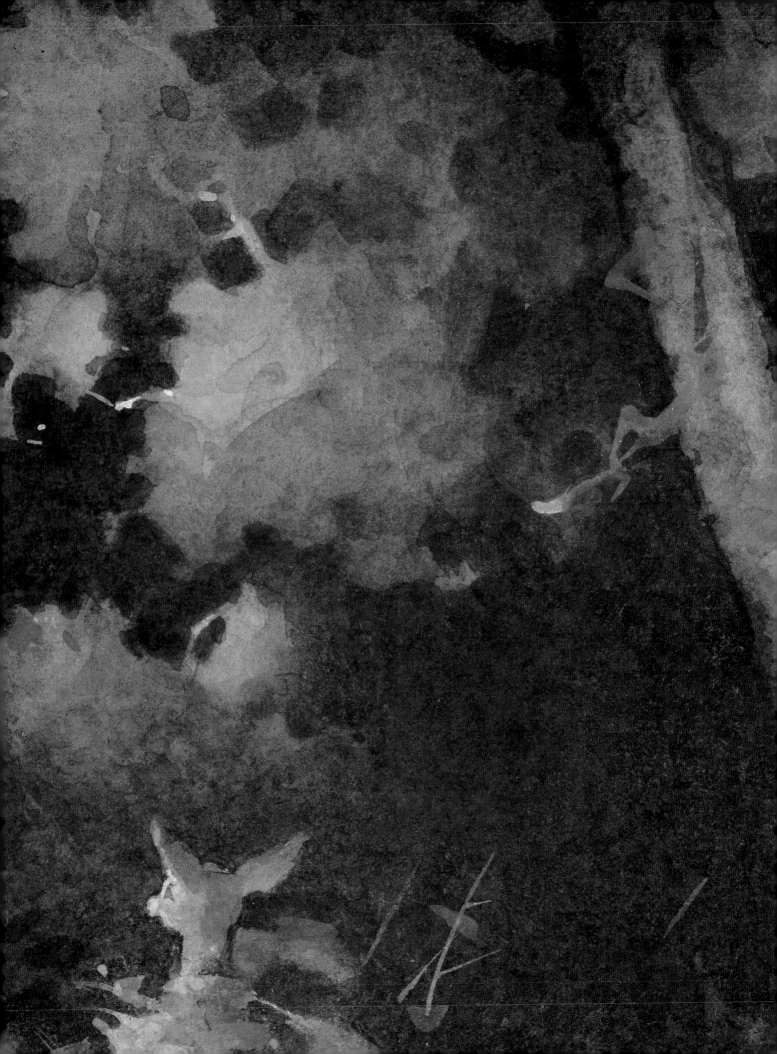

"Bir-*duh!*" *(top);* "Those are birds," explained Thumper *(above);* "BIRD!" shouted Bambi *(below).*

A long the path, Bambi and his companions came upon a flock of delighted finches who had discovered a bush full of delicious wild berries.

Bambi looked inquiringly at Thumper. "Those are birds," Thumper told him.

"B-burr?" Bambi repeated.

He hadn't had the faintest idea that the word was going to pop out of him, and neither had the rabbits. "Hey! He *talked!*" yelled Thumper. "He's trying to say 'bird'!"

"*Burr!*" Bambi said again.

"Huh-uh." Thumper never missed the chance to be instructive. He clambered up onto a rock and looked Bambi in the eye. "Say 'Bir-d,'" he ordered.

"*Burr,*" Bambi said.

"Bir-*duh!*" insisted Thumper.

This conversation had taken the finches' attention off the berries. Now they got into the act, too. "Say bird!" they peeped excitedly, darting around and around Bambi's head. "Say bird! Saybirdsaybirdsaybirdsaybird—"

28

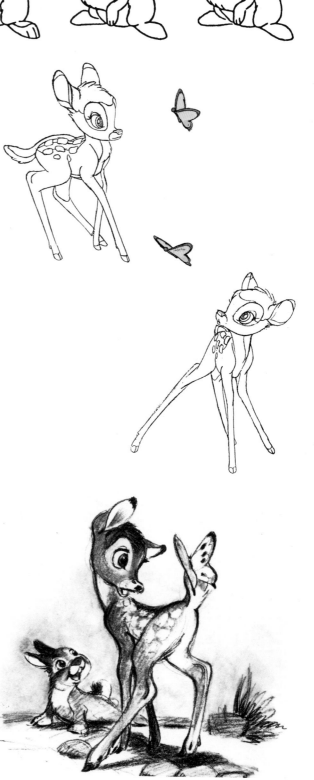

"BIRD!" shouted Bambi—so loudly that the little rabbits and finches were scattered helter-skelter. "Bird!" he repeated in delight. "Bird! Bird!"

Thumper's sisters ran back to tell their mother the news. "He talked! He talked, Mama; the young prince said 'bird.'"

"Bird, bird, bird, bird, bird," sang Bambi happily.

Just then another flying creature fluttered slowly toward Bambi—and perched on the fawn's tail.

Bambi twisted around to stare at it. "Bird!" he exclaimed happily. This bird was even more beautiful than the others!

"It's not a bird," Thumper corrected him. "It's a butterfly."

"B-butterfly?" Bambi turned around to see the butterfly again. Now it, too, was gone. But over by the rocks the ground seemed to be covered with butterflies!

Another flying creature fluttered toward Bambi *(right, middle);* "B-butterfly?" Bambi asked *(right).*

"Flower!" said Bambi proudly *(top)*; "They're flowers, pretty flowers," explained Thumper *(above)*.

He raced over to them. "Butterfly! Butterfly!" he caroled joyfully.

"No, they're flowers! Pretty flowers! See?" Thumper buried his nose in a bunch of yellow petals and sniffed appreciatively.

"Pretty fl . . ." Bambi's voice trailed off as he, too, began to sniff the flowers.

When he raised his head, he was nose-to-nose with a baby skunk.

"Flower!" said Bambi proudly.

"M-me?" The skunk's eyes widened.

He was interrupted by peals of laughter. "No, no, no, no, *no!*" gurgled Thumper, rolling around and pounding the ground deliriously. "That's not a *flower!* He's a—"

"Oh, that's all right!" the baby skunk interrupted hastily. He beamed shyly up at Bambi. "He can call me a flower if he wants to. *I* don't mind."

"Pretty!" Bambi piped again. "Pretty flower!"

From the look of pure, grateful devotion the baby skunk gave him, it was clear that Bambi had made a friend for life.

Bambi and Thumper were making their way back to their mothers when a huge crack of thunder sounded directly overhead. Startled, Bambi turned to Thumper. Was this some kind of new game, too?

But for once Thumper was looking a little uncertain. "I . . . I think I'd better go home now," he said uneasily, and vanished into the underbrush.

CRACK! came the thunder again, and a bolt of lightning sizzled in the sky. Bambi dashed, terrified, after his mother as the first raindrops began to fall.

Back at the thicket, Bambi and his mother lay down, listening to the sound of the rain. Bambi yawned, ready for sleep, but just couldn't take his eyes off the falling raindrops.

The wood mouse scurried along toward her home, stopping under toadstools whenever she could. A mother robin landed on her nest and quickly covered her three drenched fledglings with her wings.

It was dark now, but flashes of lightning kept illuminating the forest with eerie clarity. Thumper and the other rabbits huddled together under the roots of a tree and stared out fearfully at the storm. High up in his hollow tree, the owl grumbled a little and turned his back on the weather.

And as the storm passed, Bambi fell asleep beside his mother.

"He can call me a flower if he wants to." *(right, top);* A huge crack of thunder sounded overhead *(middle);* "I think I'd better go now," said Thumper *(bottom).*

A huge crack of thunder sounded directly overhead. CRACK! came the thunder again, and a bolt of lightning sizzled in the sky *(above and left)*. OPPOSITE, CLOCKWISE FROM TOP LEFT: Flashes of lightning kept illuminating the forest with an eerie clarity; Thumper and the other rabbits hid under the roots of a tree; a hummingbird flew to the shelter of a flower; Bambi couldn't take his eyes off the raindrops; the owl grumbled at the rain; and a wood mouse scurried under a toadstool.

THE MEADOW

other, what are we going to do today?" asked Bambi as he followed her through the forest. It was still so early that he could barely see her through the mist.

"I'm going to take you to the meadow," his mother replied.

Bambi paused to sniff curiously along the way, then scampered after his mother again. "Meadow? What's the meadow?" he said.

"It's a very wonderful place," his mother told him.

"Then why haven't we been there before?" asked Bambi.

"You weren't big enough," his mother replied. They were coming up to a shallow stream now, and she showed him where to cross. The instant they were across, Bambi began chattering away again.

"Mother, you know what? Thumper told me we're not the only deer in the forest!"

"Well, he's right," said his mother. "There are many deer in the forest besides us."

"Then why don't I ever *see* them?" asked the little fawn plaintively.

"You will, sometime."

Bambi was excited. "Today? On the meadow?"

"Perhaps," his mother told him. "Hush, now. We're almost there." And she led him up over a little hill.

Bambi had never seen anything like the sight that greeted him on the other side. Stretching out in front of him was what looked like a whole world's worth of long, golden-green grass studded with wildflowers. On one side of the meadow a marshy pond—so unlike the rushing streams Bambi knew from the forest—was reflecting the peach-colored light in the dawn sky. And the sky! Before this, Bambi had only caught glimpses of the sky through the trees. Out here—why, it's bigger than everything! he marveled. And I never knew the sun was as big as that, or as round!

"Meadow?" asked Bambi. "What's the meadow?" *(top);* "It's a very wonderful place." *(middle);* Stretching in front of Bambi was a whole world of long green grass *(bottom).* OPPOSITE: The meadow. OVERLEAF: Bambi had never seen anything like the sight before him.

35

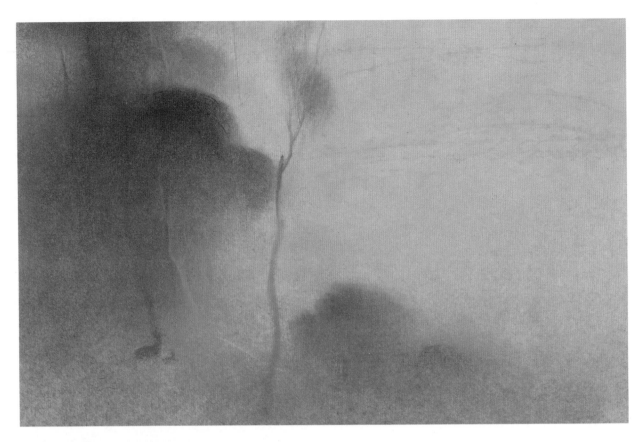

"Bambi, wait!" cried his mother. "There might be danger on the meadow." *(top);* Bambi shrank back into the underbrush *(middle);* "I'll go out first." *(bottom).*

"The *meadow!*" he cried exultingly, and raced down the slope toward it.

"No, Bambi! Wait!" In his mother's voice was a note Bambi had never heard before. She streaked ahead of him, wheeled around, and planted herself in his path.

"You must never rush out on the meadow," she panted. "There might be danger!" Then, more gently: "Out there, we are unprotected. The meadow is wide and open, and there are no trees to hide us. So we have to be very careful. Wait here."

Chastened, Bambi shrank back into the underbrush.

"I'll go out first," his mother continued. "And if the meadow is safe, I'll call you."

Only Bambi's frightened brown eyes could be seen as he huddled down in the brush and stared at his mother. Slowly and carefully, she stepped out onto the meadow and gazed across its expanse. Then she looked back at her son. "Come on, Bambi," she called. "It's all right."

Bambi crept timidly out toward her. His heart was pounding. "Come on!" his mother called. He walked hesitantly in her direction, then began to leap more courageously when suddenly she bounded away.

Startled, Bambi froze in his tracks—and then he realized that she was playing. He burst into laughter and dashed after her.

There was so much room for running on the meadow, and so much to look at! Butterflies brighter than any Bambi had seen in the forest floated leisurely above the flowers. In the sky birds soared and dove for the sheer fun of it, and in the grass Bambi found the rabbits nibbling clover.

Bambi took a mouthful but was interrupted by Thumper. "No, no, not that green stuff. Just eat the blossoms—that's the good stuff."

"Thumper!!" his mother called sternly. "What did your father tell you?"

"About what?"

"About eating the blossoms and leaving the greens," reminded his mother.

"Oh, that one." Thumper cleared his throat. "'Eating greens is a special treat . . . It makes long ears . . . And great big feet.' *But it sure is awful stuff to eat!*" he added so just Bambi could hear. "I made that last part up myself."

Bambi had chased a frog to the pond's edge when he noticed something strange. He had two reflections in the water!

Hmmm. Maybe that's just the way things happen on the meadow, he thought as he bent closer to the pond's surface. To his surprise, only one of the reflections moved. The other stayed still, staring mischievously at him.

Slowly Bambi lifted his head. There, standing next to him, was another fawn. A long-lashed, delicate-looking fawn who giggled when their eyes met.

She giggled again and stepped toward him. Bambi scrambled backwards hastily. Then, as the other fawn took another step in his direction, he turned and dashed back toward the spot where he'd last seen his mother.

To his surprise, she was standing next to another doe. "Bambi, this is your aunt Ena," she said as Bambi rushed toward her. "And that's little Faline."

There was so much room for running on the meadow *(left, above);* "No, no, not that green stuff." *(top);* "Just eat the blossoms." *(middle);* Bambi chased a frog to the pond's edge *(bottom).*

39

But Bambi didn't want anything to do with little Faline. Wide-eyed and timid, he drew back behind his mother and peeked out from around one of her legs.

For a third time, Faline giggled. "He's kind of bashful, isn't he, Mama?" she asked merrily.

"Well, maybe he wouldn't be if you'd say hello," her mother replied.

"Hello, Bambi," Faline said boldly. Bambi retreated even farther behind his mother. "I said, *hello!*"

"Aren't you going to answer her?" asked Bambi's mother.

Scowling, he shook his head.

"You're not afraid, are you?" asked his mother, and he shook his head again. "Well, then, go ahead!" And she pushed him with her nose. "Go on, say hello," she told him firmly, in a motherly, no-nonsense voice.

Bambi cleared his throat. He pawed the ground a little. Then he glowered up at Faline. "H'lo," he croaked.

That was all it took. The silly young Faline giggled and danced around Bambi, who was so shy and confused by her that he fell into a small pond.

Faline darted in and out of the pond's cattails, giving Bambi little kisses on his cheeks. Finally, forgetting his shyness, Bambi gave a surprising whoop and charged after her.

He had two reflections on the water *(top);* Standing next to him was another fawn *(middle);* She giggled and stepped toward him *(bottom).*

40

Bambi dashed back to his mother *(above)*; Bambi cleared his throat. "H'lo," he croaked *(right, top)*; Faline gave Bambi little kisses *(middle)*; Silly young Faline giggled and danced around Bambi *(below)*.

They were plunging back and forth across the meadow and leaping fearlessly off the highest boulders *(top);* Then the bucks grew still *(middle);* Bambi was in the presence of majesty *(bottom).*

Bambi and Faline were playing tag when they heard a low, thudding sound. They paused. Could this be another thunderstorm?

No. Streaking out of the woods were more deer. Dozens of huge deer—bigger than Bambi could have dreamed. The thudding sound was the noise of their hoofs.

Bambi stared at the bucks with awe. They were plunging back and forth across the meadow, leaping fearlessly off the highest boulders and grappling in play-combat. He could hardly believe he would ever grow into something so magnificent. Bambi began to show off with his own imitation of their leaps.

Then—as he watched—the bucks grew still. As one, they turned to face the woods. They had all sensed someone coming.

It was a mighty stag, far bigger than the rest, with massive antlers fully a yard across. And something about the grave, unhurried way the stag moved toward the meadow told Bambi without any words that he was in the presence of majesty.

Slowly, proudly, the stag advanced and walked up to the group of bucks without seeming to notice them. He was about to pass on by when instead he turned his great head and stared down at little Bambi in silence.

Bambi stared back, frozen with awe. Then he smiled hesitantly at the huge stag.

Streaking out of the forest were dozens of huge deer *(top and middle);* Bambi began to show off with imitations of their leaps *(below)*.

Then Bambi smiled hesitantly *(top);* "He's known as the Great Prince of the Forest. He's very brave and very wise." *(middle and bottom).*

Not a flicker of expression crossed the stag's face. Only his ears twitched a little, as if he were surprised at Bambi's daring.

Bambi's smile faded away, and he felt himself growing shy again without knowing why. The stag continued his slow, stately procession through the meadow and did not look back.

Suddenly Bambi became aware that his mother had walked up behind him. "Mother, he stopped and looked at me," he whispered.

"Yes, I know."

"Mother, why was everyone still when he came onto the meadow?"

"Everyone respects him," his mother explained softly. "For of all the deer in the forest, not one has lived half so long. He's very brave—and very wise. That's why he's known as the Great Prince of the Forest." She turned to watch the stag as he walked away.

T he old stag looked down on the meadow from a high ledge. He moved deeper into the forest, then halted, sensing something was wrong. Suddenly he turned and raced back through the forest and onto the meadow.

Bambi saw the Great Prince charging back toward the other deer as if to warn them. Above him, a flock of crows was screaming crazily in the sky.

Before Bambi could ask what was the matter, the other deer were crashing past him, running toward the forest.

"Faline!" Bambi heard Ena scream, and Faline raced up to her mother's side. The two of them dashed out of sight. A panic-stricken pheasant whirred up into the air directly in front of Bambi. All about him were the thundering of deer hoofs and the screams of terrified birds.

Where was everyone going? Why was everyone frightened? Where was his mother?

The little fawn stood stock-still in the grass, watching bewilderedly as the other deer hurtled past him. "Bambi!" he heard his mother calling from far away—but so many creatures were blocking his view that he couldn't see her.

"Mother!" he called desperately. "Mother, where are you?"

No answer.

"Mother!" Bambi screamed.

Then—without any warning—the great stag was at his side. Together they raced toward the edge of the forest, where Bambi's mother caught up to them. The three deer dashed to safety just as a shattering explosion rang through the air.

Then the only sounds on the meadow were the echo of the shot and the crows' screams.

All about him were the screams of terrified birds *(top);* Suddenly, the Great Prince raced back through the forest and onto the meadow *(above).*

Bambi heard his mother calling (above and right); Without any warning the stag was by his side (below).

I t was sunset before Bambi's mother felt it was safe to come out of hiding. "Come on out, Bambi," she said gently.

Bambi didn't budge from his spot deep in-side the thicket.

"Come on," she urged. "It's safe now. We don't have to hide any longer."

Bambi poked his head out cautiously. When he saw that all was still, he pulled himself out of the thicket little by little and walked, trem-bling, up to his mother.

"What happened, Mother? Why did we all run?" he asked in a shaky voice.

After a long pause she said quietly, "Man was in the forest."

Suddenly the air seemed very cold.

Together they raced toward the edge of the forest *(top);* It was sunset before his mother felt it was safe to come out *(middle and bottom).*

WINTER

To Bambi, each golden summer day was like the ones that had come before. Autumn crept in so gradually that year that he hardly noticed the trees changing colors until they began to lose their leaves. First one scarlet maple leaf tore itself loose, then a handful of yellow oak leaves—and then it seemed to Bambi that the whole forest was filled with scraps of color dancing in the wind.

Bambi was sure that the last two leaves on the oak tree just outside his thicket meant to stay put forever. Each morning he ran to see whether they were still there, and each morning they were still fluttering bravely on their branch. One day, though, Bambi glanced up to see the smaller of the two leaves shuddering in the breeze. With a sound like a sigh, it broke loose and floated gently to the ground. Only a few seconds later its companion drifted down to lie beside it.

The next morning Bambi woke up early, with a sense that something had changed in the night. The air was frosty and cold, and the thicket was filled with a strange bluish-white light. He went to the thicket's opening to explore—and gasped.

"Mother, look!" he cried. "What's all that white stuff?"

His mother lifted her head. "Why, it's snow!" she said in surprise.

"Snow?" asked Bambi, staring at the brand-new forest.

"Yes," his mother told him. "Winter has come."

Bambi took a cautious step into the white drift outside the thicket. "Look. Footprints!" he said in delight.

Just then, Thumper called from a nearby snow-covered hill.

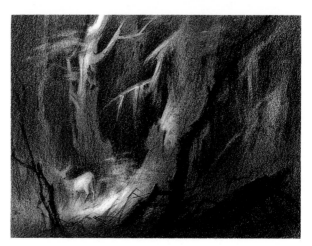

Autumn crept in so gradually, Bambi hardly noticed *(top);* First one leaf tore itself loose, then a handful *(middle);* The air was frosty and cold *(bottom).* OPPOSITE: The last two leaves fluttered bravely.

"Mother! What's all that white stuff?" *(top);* Bambi took a cautious step into the white drift *(above);* "Hi ya, Bambi. Watch what I can do." *(below and right).* OPPOSITE: "I guess you'd better unwind it," volunteered Thumper *(top);* "Ya gotta watch both ends at the same time." *(right, middle);* "Look, the water's stiff." *(bottom).*

"Hi ya, Bambi! Watch what I can do. Yippee!" He ran down the hill, leaped out onto the water, which was no longer water but ice, and slid far out on the pond. "C'mon, it's all right. Look, the water's stiff."

But when Bambi took a mighty leap from the same hill, his "Yippee" abruptly ended in an "Ooof!" and he wound up on his belly.

Thumper called out to him, "Some fun, huh, Bambi?"

Bambi responded with a very weak smile. Try as he might, he could not stand on the slippery surface, and his attempts gave Thumper a bad case of the giggles.

Through his laughter Thumper managed to say, "No, no! Ya gotta watch both ends at the same time." He decided it was time for him to take charge.

First Thumper pushed one of Bambi's legs up and then another, then another and another until Bambi stood shakily. But Bambi's legs would not stay put and down he went again. This time his legs got all tied up.

"I guess you'd better unwind it," Thumper volunteered.

Again Thumper got all of Bambi's legs in position, and giving him a good push, together they slid across the ice. For a moment, Thumper's plan seemed to be working, but not for long. Smack! They slid into the biggest snowbank.

As Thumper's head popped up out of the snow, he heard a tiny whistling noise coming from a burrow in the side of a hill. Curious,

Curious, they headed over to see what it was *(top)*; "Is it spring yet?" murmured Flower dreamily *(middle)*; The days grew shorter and the snow deeper *(bottom)*. OPPOSITE: Bambi's mother tore bark off a tree and offered it to him *(top)*; For hours every day they struggled in search of scraps of bark and twigs *(bottom)*.

they headed over to see what it was—and found Flower, the skunk, lying on his back in a nest of leaves, sound asleep and snoring.

"Wake up, wake up!" said Thumper.

Flower opened a drowsy eye. "Is it spring yet?" he murmured dreamily.

"*Spring!*" said Bambi incredulously. "Winter's just starting!"

"Mmmmm-hmmmmm," sighed Flower.

"Whatcha doin'?" asked the curious Thumper. "Hibernatin'?"

"Mmmmm-hmmmmm," said Flower again.

"Whatcha want to do that for?" asked Bambi.

Flower chuckled a little. "All us flowers sleep in the winter," he said with a yawn. "Well, g'night . . ."

He pulled his fluffy tail over himself like a quilt, snuggled down into the leaves, and went back to sleep.

As the days grew shorter and the snow grew deeper, winter stopped being fun and became wearisome. Now it seemed to Bambi as though he were always limping along through the snowdrifts, always trying to catch up to the rest of the deer, always fighting the icy wind, always hungry and cold.

The deer in the forest had banded together to look for food. For hours every day they struggled through the woods in search of the scraps of bark and twigs that were all the forest offered them now.

When Bambi's mother had first torn a piece of bark off a tree and gave it to him, he had been shocked at how dry and tasteless it was. "I can't eat this, Mother!" he cried. "It's awful!"

"You must get used to it, Bambi," was her answer. "It won't seem so bad after a while."

And when even the bark grew scarce, Bambi realized that his mother had been right. Sometimes the two of them could only find enough for one. When that happened, his mother always went without.

Then came the day when they found no bark at all. In every direction, every tree they could see had been stripped higher than Bambi's mother could reach.

"It's no use, dear," she said at last, dropping back onto all fours. "Let's go back to the thicket. We'll try again tomorrow."

Back in the thicket, Bambi curled up wearily next to his mother. "Winter sure is long, isn't it?" he said with a shiver.

"It seems long, but it won't last forever." His mother comforted him.

"I'm awfully hungry, Mother," whispered Bambi.

His mother kissed him. "Yes, dear, I know," she said patiently. "Go to sleep now. Things will be better in the morning."

So the weeks passed by, lean and bitter, until one morning Bambi's mother called happily, "Bambi, come here!" They had wandered to the meadow that morning, and she was standing near the brook staring down at something in the snow.

Bambi scampered over. There in the snow was a patch of green!

"New spring grass," said his mother.

Bambi took an eager mouthful, and then another and another. The grass tasted of spring itself—fresh, vibrant, leafy. It was a flavor he had almost forgotten after so many days of hard, dry bark. Bambi ate hungrily.

Bambi's mother had barely started to eat when abruptly she stopped and lifted her head to sniff the air. She glanced from side to side as if she were trying to hear something. "Bambi," she whispered. But he was so busy eating that he didn't hear her.

"Bambi!" she said in terror.

Startled, Bambi looked up at her.

"The thicket!" she cried, and the two of them sprang toward the forest.

Bambi had never run so fast. He vaulted over the stream without thinking about it and dashed across the snow. He could hear his mother pounding along just behind him, her breath coming hard. "Faster!" she called out. "Faster, Bambi!"

A shot rang out.

Horrified, Bambi glanced back over his shoulder at his mother. "Keep running!" she cried hoarsely. "Don't look back!"

Another shot echoed in the air just as he reached the edge of the woods. He leaped forward, darting through the trees, and with a final burst of energy, tore through the underbrush, down the last steps of the old, familiar path, and into the thicket. There he stopped, gasping for breath.

"We . . . we made it, Mother!" he panted. "We made it!"

There was no answer.

"Mother?" Bambi faltered.

Silence.

"The thicket!" she cried and the two of them sprang forward *(top);* "Faster, faster!" *(above);* "Don't look back!" *(left).* Opposite: "Go to sleep now. Things will be better in the morning." *(top);* There in the snow was a patch of green *(middle);* "Bambi!" she said in terror *(bottom).* Preceding overleaf: The weeks passed, lean and bitter.

"Mother?" Bambi faltered. Silence. "Mother!" *(above);* The forest had become dark and ominous. The trees seemed bigger and taller and less friendly *(below).*

Bambi walked to the entrance of the thicket and peeked out into the woods.

There was no sign of his mother.

"Mother!" Bambi cried again. "Mother, where are you?"

A light snow was beginning to fall. Trembling, Bambi cautiously left the thicket. His mother was nowhere in sight.

Where could she be? He knew she was out there somewhere. Why didn't she answer?

"Mother!"

The forest had become dark and ominous. The trees seemed bigger and taller and less friendly. The snow was coming down harder now. Bambi tried to retrace his steps, but his tracks were already completely covered. In the muffled silence of the new snow, there was no sound other than his bewildered cries.

He called again and again, "Mother . . . Mother!" Desperately Bambi searched for her, stumbling through the snowfall that was now so dense he could scarcely see where he was going. His heart was beating so hard that

he could not think. He had never known fear like this before, or such loneliness.

"Mother," he wept, and his head bent low.

His last cry froze in his throat and became a startled gasp.

A huge, dark shape loomed above him. It was the old stag Bambi had once seen on the meadow—the Great Prince of the Forest. He was staring down at the little fawn, his face hidden in shadow.

"Your mother can't be with you anymore," he said quietly.

Bambi gave one wild, beseeching glance up at the stag. Then, stricken, he bowed his head. A single tear rolled down his cheek and vanished into the snow.

"Come, my son," said the stag.

He turned and walked back into the forest.

Bambi looked once—only once—toward the spot where he had last seen his mother. Then, slowly, he began to follow the Great Prince into the soft snow.

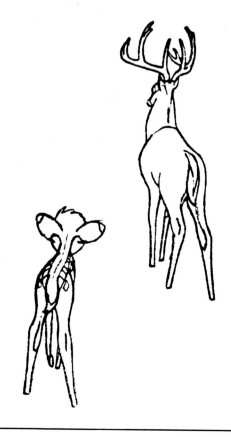

Bambi's cry became a startled gasp *(above);* A dark shape loomed above him *(right, top);* "Come, my son," said the stag *(middle);* Slowly he began to follow the Great Prince *(bottom).*

SPRING

Winter had come and gone three times and now once again the last patches of snow had melted reluctantly away. The plants in the forest—freed from winter's icy grasp—were springing joyously into life. Sun poured through the new leaves and splashed down onto the wildflowers. The trees were filled with blossoms and birds, the air with fragrance and birdsong. There wasn't a crevice or a cranny in the forest that spring had left untouched.

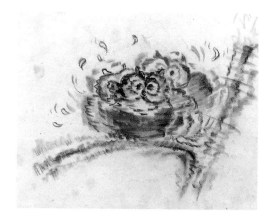

Not that any of this pleased the old owl, who despised spring. He hated all the sunlight and the twittering and the way every tree he tried to take a nap in was filled with love-struck birds.

"Same thing every spring," he grumbled. "Tweet-tweet, tweet-tweet, tweet-tweet! Love's sweet song, huh? Pain in the pin-feathers, *I* call it . . . What's that? What's that? Oh, *now* what's going on?"

The sapling he was perched in had suddenly begun to vibrate as though an earthquake were shaking it. It flung the surprised owl right off his perch.

He landed with a feather-shaking thump on a branch below. "Ouch!" he yelled. "Stop it! Get out of here! All of you!" Crossly he peered down at the handsome, broad-shouldered young buck who had been polishing his antlers against the tree trunk. "And you, too," he added, almost falling off his branch again.

At the sight of the owl, the young buck broke into a smile. "Hello, Friend Owl!" he called gaily. "Don't you remember me?"

Top to bottom: *"Now* what's going on?"; A broad-shouldered buck was polishing his antlers; "Get out of here! All of you!" yelled the owl; "And you, too," he added. Opposite: Sun poured through the new leaves.

"Why, it's the young prince, Bambi!" *(top);*
"Hello, Bambi." It was Thumper! *(above);*
"Hi ya, fellas." They turned to see Flower
(below).

"Why . . . why . . . why, it's the young prince!" gasped the owl, his frown vanishing completely.

Bambi nodded.

"I see you've traded in your spots for a pair of antlers," observed the owl, and Bambi lifted his head proudly. "Very impressive. You know, just the other day I was wondering what had become of you."

"Hello, Bambi!" called an eager voice, cutting short the owl's pleasantries. "I thought that might be you!"

It was Thumper! But this Thumper was just as changed as Bambi himself. Gone were the baby roundness of his face and the fluffiness of his little body. He was trim, lean, and sleek now—the perfect specimen of a wild rabbit.

As the two friends greeted each other, they heard another voice calling, "Hi ya, fellas!" They turned to see Flower waving at them from a patch of daisies. He, too, had grown up, but his smile was as sweet as ever. He was just as bashful as ever, too. When Bambi and Thumper turned toward him, he dropped his head shyly and began sniffing the daisies as though that was what he'd been meaning to do all along.

J ust then a pair of meadowlarks flew playfully past Flower, zooming around his head almost making him dizzy. The birds chased each other around Bambi's new antlers and played tag over Thumper's head for just a moment before spinning gaily in circles and darting away again.

"Well, what's the matter with *them?*" Flower asked in amazement. "Why are they acting that way?"

"Don't you *know?*" the owl asked them. The three friends shook their heads. "They're twitterpated!" the owl explained.

"*Twitterpated?*" echoed Bambi.

"Nearly everybody gets twitterpated in the springtime!" said the owl. Bambi, Thumper, and Flower stared blankly at him, so he explained further.

"You're walking along, minding your own business—looking neither to the left nor to the right—when all of a sudden, you run smack into a pretty face. *Hoo-hoo!*"

The owl's voice was dripping with sarcasm.

"You begin to get weak in the knees," he continued. "Your head's in a whirl. And before you know it, you're walking on air!"

He glowered down at them. "Knocks you for a loop, it does! And you completely lose your head . . . and it can happen to anybody, so you'd better be careful!"

He aimed a cranky wing at Bambi. "It could happen to you." He pointed at Thumper. "To you, too." He pointed at Flower—and hesitated.

"Well, what's the matter with *them?*" asked Flower, watching a pair of meadowlarks *(top);* "They're twitterpated!" *(above).*

"You're walking along, minding your own business—looking neither to the left nor to the right—when all of a sudden you run smack into a pretty face. Knocks you for a loop, it does! And you completely lose your head."

"Yes, it could even happen to you," the owl decided after a second. "So you'd all better watch out!"

"Well, it's *not* going to happen to me," said Thumper firmly.

"Me neither," agreed Bambi.

"Me *neither!*" said Flower with great force.

And with that the three friends marched off into the forest, each of them utterly determined to resist the charms of spring.

But, as Flower passed a blossoming bush, he thought he heard it giggle. He hesitated . . . he peered into the bush . . . he couldn't believe it, but . . . the bush was blinking back at him. He started to run after Bambi and Thumper, but the bush giggled again.

Then a pretty girl skunk came out of the bush and with a whirling dance gave the startled Flower a kiss.

Flower was completely twitterpated. He giggled, shrugged his shoulders, and went off happily through the field of daisies with his new girlfriend.

Thumper and Bambi were shocked as they watched the two skunk tails disappear together in the distance.

The bush was blinking back at him *(top)*, Flower was completely twitterpated *(middle)*; Two skunk tails disappeared together in the distance *(bottom).*

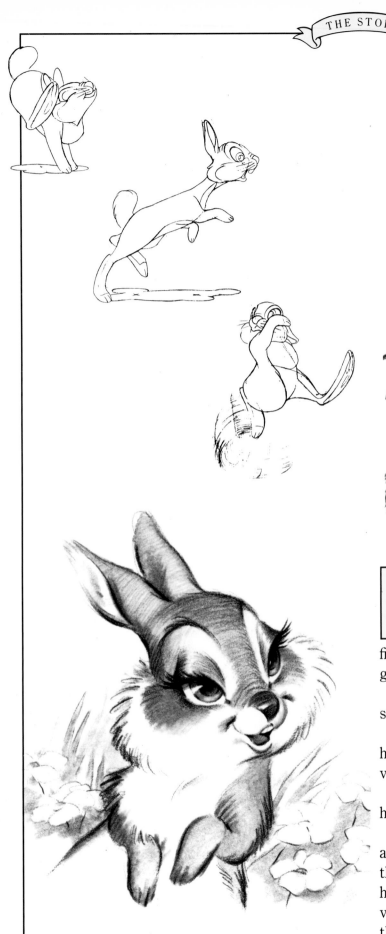

I n the forest glade ahead, a lovely girl bunny was preening herself. When she saw Thumper approaching . . . well, it was love at first sight. She cleared her throat prettily to get Thumper's attention as he went by.

Thumper stopped in midstride and just stared at her with his mouth open.

She began humming a song, then fluttered her eyelashes, and said in a sultry, musical voice, "Hello."

Thumper swallowed hard and said nothing; he was too twitterpated to respond at all.

Bambi was appalled at Thumper's behavior and kept walking, leaving him behind under the girl bunny's magic spell. Bambi could hear her singing to Thumper in her soft, seductive voice, "Lah, lah, lah, lah . . ." and he could tell that Thumper loved every bit of it.

In the forest glade, a lovely girl bunny was preening herself *(left);* She sang to him in her soft, seductive voice, "Lah, lah, lah . . ." and Thumper loved every bit of it *(below).* OPPOSITE: Thumper stopped in midstride and just stared with his mouth open *(top, left and right);* She began humming a song, then fluttered her eyelashes, and said, "Hello." *(bottom).*

FALINE

Bambi sighed as he walked slowly toward a stream to take a drink. *I guess Friend Owl was right—at least about them,* Bambi thought scornfully, bending his head to drink. *I'm certainly not going to . . .*

Suddenly he choked on a mouthful of water. There, in the stream, was another reflection. This time Bambi knew it certainly wasn't his.

He lifted his head slowly. Gazing at him with a faint smile on her face was a slender, graceful young doe.

"Hello, Bambi," she said. "Don't you remember me?"

Bambi only stared at her, open-mouthed.

"I'm Faline."

Faline! Bambi hadn't seen her in months. How could this beautiful creature be the fawn he had chased on the meadow so long ago?

Still smiling, Faline advanced across the stream toward him.

He took a hasty step backward and tripped over a rock in the stream. *Splash!* He collapsed in a gawky heap and stared up at Faline.

Her smile didn't waver. She looked breathtakingly composed as she continued across the stream toward Bambi.

"I . . . I . . ." Bambi stammered. He gathered himself up and clambered backward up the bank of the stream.

He might have gotten away, too, if his brand-new antlers hadn't become tangled in the branch of an apple tree.

Pink petals showered gently down as Bambi shook his head frantically, trying to free himself. But before he'd made any progress, Faline walked up to him, pushed the branch aside, and kissed him on the cheek.

Bambi caught his breath. He turned his head toward Faline and stared into her huge, dark eyes.

"Hello, Bambi," Faline said. "Don't you remember me?" *(top);* Bambi only stared at her, open-mouthed *(middle);* Faline walked up to him and kissed him gently on the cheek *(bottom).* OPPOSITE: Could this be the fawn he had chased on the meadow so long ago?

So . . . so . . . so this is what Friend Owl was talking about, thought Bambi dazedly. The forest suddenly seemed to Bambi like a cloud-filled sky and he felt as though he could fly.

Faline scampered across the stream, paused to look back at Bambi teasingly, then sprang up the bank.

Bambi leaped after her, and the two of them bounded off through the forest.

So, this is what the owl was talking about, thought Bambi *(left)*; The forest seemed like a cloud-filled sky *(below)*.

Suddenly someone thrust himself between them. It was another buck. He was bigger than Bambi and heavier. He scowled fiercely at Bambi and shook his antlers threateningly.

"Ronno!" Bambi gasped.

Bambi remembered Ronno from the year before. He was older than Bambi and Faline, and was a horrible bully.

Now he was glowering at Bambi. "She belongs to me," he said, and began pushing Faline up the path into the forest.

"Bambi!" cried a frightened Faline.

"Leave her alone!" Bambi ordered. He couldn't help feeling frightened himself. For as long as he'd known Ronno, the other deer had always taken anything he wanted.

Now Ronno turned and gave Bambi an ugly grin. "What are you going to do about it, *little prince?*" he taunted.

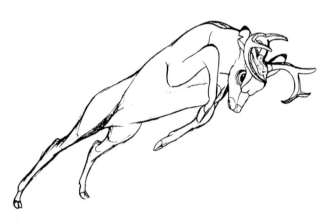

Suddenly anger blazed through Bambi and burned his fear completely away. He began to paw the ground with his hoof.

Ronno laughed sneeringly. He pawed the ground himself and thundered toward Bambi. They grappled antlers for only a second before Ronno flung the younger buck over his shoulder.

"Bambi!" cried Faline in alarm.

Bambi hit the ground with a bone-shaking thud. For a minute he lay there motionless, the wind knocked out of him. Then, as Ronno charged toward him again, he staggered to his feet and aimed his antlers at Ronno's chest. Again they grappled and again Ronno threw Bambi into the air.

Bambi pulled himself up painfully and stood on his hind legs as Ronno charged. This time the bucks fought with their front hoofs, slashing viciously at each other while a trembling Faline watched. At first she was sure Ronno was going to win the battle. But, little by little, the bigger buck began to tire. He had never before had to fight so long or so hard.

Suddenly, someone thrust himself between them *(top)*; Ronno pawed the ground and thundered toward Bambi *(middle)*; "Bambi!" cried Faline in alarm *(bottom)*. OVERLEAF: Suddenly, anger blazed through Bambi and burned his fear away. Ronno charged toward him again, and again they grappled.

This time the bucks fought with their front hoofs, while a trembling Faline watched *(top);* They were fighting on the edge of a rain-filled gully now *(above).*

He's starting to give up! Bambi exulted as he pushed Ronno backward yet again. They were fighting on the edge of a rain-filled gully now. Bambi gritted his teeth and hurled himself into the air, hitting Ronno with the whole of his weight.

Ronno stumbled backward and lost his footing. With a furious shout he tumbled head over heels down the gully and into the water.

Ronno shook his head as if to clear it. Then, slowly, he rose and gave Bambi a bewildered look. He shook his head again and stumbled away through the water.

Faline tiptoed up to Bambi's side. She laid her head lovingly on his shoulder. And together they walked through the mists out onto the beauty of the meadow.

With a furious shout Ronno tumbled head over heels down the side of the gully *(clockwise from top)*; Faline tiptoed up to Bambi's side *(above)*. OVERLEAF: Together they walked through the mists.

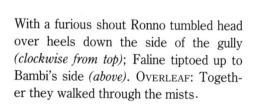

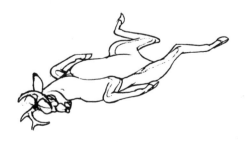

Danger in the Forest

O ne chilly gray autumn dawn, Bambi woke up with a start. Faline was still sleeping peacefully beside him in the thicket. None of the birds were awake yet, and except for a few falling leaves, the woods seemed still. Yet Bambi was sure there was something wrong. He stood up quietly, so as not to wake Faline, and stepped cautiously out of the thicket.

The forest was silent and calm, but now Bambi knew what had awakened him. It was the smell of smoke.

Moving more quickly, he trotted up a narrow path that led to a cliff. From the cliff, he knew, there was a clear view of the valley.

And there below, a thin, curling line of smoke was rising from a campfire.

"It is Man," came a deep, grave voice from behind Bambi. He turned and saw the old stag, the Great Prince of the Forest, standing beside him. As if in answer to the Great Prince's words, crows circling in the valley below began screaming raucously.

"Man is here again," said the old stag. "There are many this time. We must go deep into the forest. Come with me!"

Before Bambi could speak, the stag had wheeled around and dashed into the woods.

Bambi took a tentative step after him and then stopped. "Faline!" he cried aloud. "I've got to get Faline!"

In the thicket, the sound of the crows had awakened Faline. She looked around nervously for Bambi. Where had he gone? She, too, sensed something in the air.

She called frantically for Bambi several times and searched for him near the thicket. But there was no answer.

With each passing moment she became more frightened. Finally she ran in panic through the woods.

Bambi stepped cautiously out of the thicket *(top);* From the cliff, Bambi knew there was a clear view of the valley below *(middle);* The sound of crows had awakened Faline *(bottom).* OPPOSITE: In the middle of the river was an island of refuge.

"Man is here again," said the old stag *(top)*; "Faline!" Bambi cried aloud. "I've got to get Faline!" *(above)*.

Bambi reached the thicket only seconds after Faline had left. He was beside himself with fear for his loved one, and he darted off in search of her.

T he crows were above the treetops now. Their harsh shrieks of warning were beginning to wake up the whole forest. Eyes glanced up uneasily, and a few nervous forest creatures began creeping deeper into the woods, hardly daring to peek over their shoulders to see what was happening.

But everyone knew what was happening. The crows' screams of danger could mean only one thing.

The meadow was hushed and fearful. Three pheasants trembled in their hiding place under the deep grass. "He's coming," faltered the youngest of the three.

"Hush! Don't get excited!" her older sister tried to soothe her.

"He's . . . he's coming closer!" wailed the first pheasant, unheeding. "We'd better fly!"

"No! Don't fly!" gasped the other two pheasants. "Whatever you do, don't fly!"

The first pheasant was sobbing now. "He's almost here!" she wept, and her voice rose to a scream. "I can't stand it any longer!" Wings

The crows' shrieks were beginning to wake up the whole forest *(above)*; "He's coming closer! We'd better fly!" *(left)*; Wings beating wildly, she threw herself into the air *(below)*; Instantly the shooting began in force *(bottom)*.

beating wildly, she threw herself into the air.

There was a thunderous crack overhead, and her body fell from the sky.

Instantly the shooting began in force.

The animals hidden under the grass panicked at the sound. Terrified, they streaked across the meadow toward the forest. Birds flew shrieking into the sky—and dropped motionless out of it. The sound of gunshots came ever closer, and with it the crazed barking of the hunting dogs.

The crows were above the treetops now. OPPOSITE: Eyes glanced up uneasily, and a few nervous creatures began scurrying deeper into the woods *(top);* Searching desperately for Bambi, Faline dashed up a rocky path *(bottom).*

Faline ran and ran, the dogs biting at her heels *(above and below)*.

Searching desperately for Bambi, Faline dashed up a rocky path. Suddenly, she turned and ran back in the other direction, chased by a large pack of snarling, barking dogs—Man's dogs.

Faline ran and ran, the dogs biting at her heels. They seemed to be everywhere, and Faline's only hope was to clamber up onto a high rocky ledge just out of their reach.

"Bambi!" she cried frantically, "Bambi!"

The dogs yapped and growled, all the while leaping up at her.

In the distance, Bambi heard the ominous howling and barking of the dogs and above the noise, Faline's terrified voice. He followed his senses to the spot where the vicious dogs had Faline cornered and without a moment's hesitation, he plunged into battle.

With lowered head and strong thrusts, Bambi flipped one of the dogs over his antlers, but the rest of the snarling mass instantly turned on him.

The dogs seemed to be everywhere *(left, top)*, and Faline's only hope was to clamber up onto a rocky ledge just out of their reach *(right, top);* Bambi followed his senses to the spot where the vicious dogs had Faline cornered *(above)*.

With lowered head and strong thrusts, Bambi flipped one of the dogs over his antlers, but the rest of the snarling mass instantly turned on him.

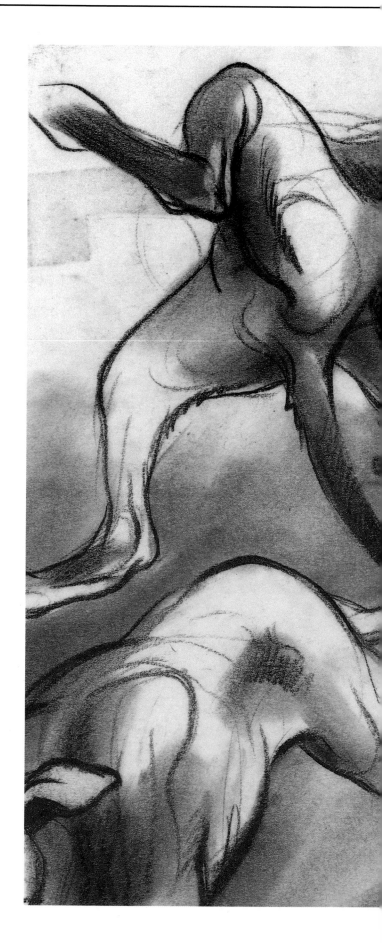

He gathered his strength and sailed out over the chasm *(top);* Without a moment's hesitation, Bambi plunged into battle *(above, left);* Faline leaped off the ledge and disappeared into the forest *(above).*

Bambi retreated a few paces—but only to charge again. This time he used his hoofs too, kicking wildly as he stabbed with his antlers. He reared up violently, shaking the dogs off, and then whirled around to attack again.

"Quick, Faline! Jump!" he called.

Faline leaped off the ledge and disappeared into the forest.

Bambi continued to fight valiantly, until finally he saw his opportunity to break away. He dashed up the steep bank behind the rocky ledge. The dogs were so close behind him that Bambi could feel their breath on his heels. He pulled himself up the bank with every bit of strength he had. The pack of dogs would certainly have reached him and torn him apart, if the frantic pawing of his hoofs hadn't started a rockslide as he neared the top of the bank.

Now Bambi could hear the dogs' agonized yelps as rocks and boulders pelted them. But he didn't slow down. Ahead of him was a gorge. On the other side, he would be safe . . . He gathered his strength and sailed out over the chasm.

A shot rang out and Bambi's body arched in agony. Then he hit the ground on the other side and sprawled there, unconscious.

A shot rang out and Bambi's body arched in agony. He hit the ground and sprawled there, unconscious.

Down in the valley, a passing breeze blew a handful of dry leaves onto the dying campfire. Soon a tiny flame sprang up and began licking at the grass. One second, it seemed, there was a forest. The next second, there was nothing but fire. The flames devoured everything they touched and, ravenous for more, rushed forward into the woods. Trees that had stood for hundreds of years groaned as the fire consumed them. Blazing embers fell into the stream and set it boiling. And hundreds upon hundreds of desperate animals raced only inches ahead of the flickering demon that was so eager to catch them.

Bambi knew nothing of this. He was lying in a haze of pain at the edge of the gorge. Dimly he was aware of the heat and smoke, the crackling of the flames and the animals' screams, but none of it mattered to him.

Soon a tiny flame sprang up *(top)*; Hundreds of animals raced inches ahead of the flames *(middle)*; Dimly, Bambi was aware of the heat and smoke *(bottom)*; "Get up, Bambi." *(right)*.

Then he heard a deep voice above him. "Get up, Bambi."

Bambi's eyelids flickered, but he didn't move.

"You must get up," repeated the voice.

This time Bambi raised his head and stared dully at the Great Prince standing over him. Bambi tried to rise, but fell to the ground.

"You must," said the stag sternly.

Bambi didn't answer.

"*Get up!*" The stag's voice was harsh now. Bambi managed to pull himself shakily onto his knees. He was staggering so badly that he pitched forward. Pain coursed through his body. He would have collapsed again if the old stag hadn't been there.

"Follow me," commanded the stag, and Bambi began stumbling along behind him.

Then a sheet of fire raised itself up in front of the two deer. The scorching blast of heat cleared the pain from Bambi's head. Now he understood the danger they were in. He skidded along the gorge behind the stag, all thoughts of his injury forgotten.

> One second, it seemed, there was a forest. The next, there was nothing but fire *(top);* Bambi tried to rise, but fell to the ground *(middle and bottom).*

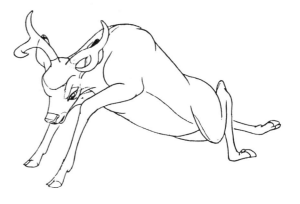

91

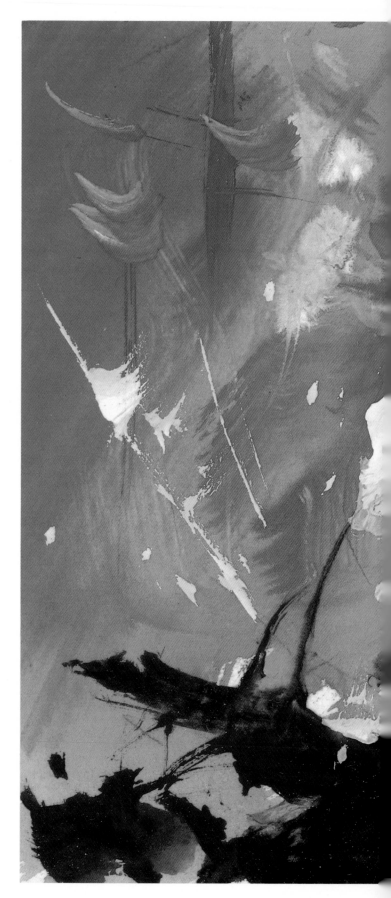

But everywhere the two deer turned, the mocking flames rose up in front of them.

"The stream!" called the stag. "It's our only hope!"

He wheeled around in the thick smoke and led Bambi to the stream.

Huge tree trunks, glowing red, were toppling into the water all around them. Sizzling embers flew through the air like burning brands.

This is the wrong direction! We're heading toward the waterfall! thought Bambi frantically. But looking backward, he realized they had no choice. Behind them was a solid wall of fire.

The noise of the waterfall was drowning out even the sound of the flames. Bambi and the stag rushed ahead over the slippery rocks. The current was stronger here and it swept them along. He could barely stand.

Now they came to the very edge of the waterfall. Twenty feet below them, water churned and boiled furiously above the treacherous rocks.

The two deer hesitated, but only for a second. Then they threw themselves over the edge and fell into the maelstrom below.

A mile or so downstream, the water became wide and calm, though tinged with the reflections of flames leaping high into the air. In the middle of the river there was a tiny island where the creatures of the forest were taking refuge.

Animals who had never touched water except to drink it were swimming carefully across the river now. A possum came slowly toward shore, her babies hanging upside down from her tail like a row of ornaments. Mrs.

Looking back, Bambi realized they had no choice. Behind them was a solid wall of fire.

Raccoon laid the last baby of her damp brood down on the sandy bank and began licking its fur to warm it. "I know it seems strange here," she whispered to her children, "but we're safe. And tomorrow we'll be able to go back home."

But what would be left of their home?

Faline was standing at one end of the island, watching the water anxiously. Since she had fled from the dogs, she had seen no sign of Bambi. Surely no animals could still be alive in the forest, and it seemed like hours since she had crossed the water herself . . .

Then she gave a gasp of relief. Coming slowly across the river were the Great Prince and Bambi.

Bambi had no idea whether Faline had made it to safety. His wound was beginning to ache again and he was conscious of how very tired he was.

Just a little farther, he told himself as he struggled along searching the shoreline hopefully. Just a . . . little farther . . .

"Bambi!" called Faline eagerly.

Bambi looked up and met her eyes. A burst of joy surged through him. She was safe!

His pain and exhaustion vanished, and he swam the last few yards easily. Then he was on shore, standing once again next to Faline.

Bambi gazed silently into her eyes. There were no words for what he was feeling. He and Faline leaned wearily against each other and turned together to watch the forest. Above the remains of the trees, the sky was burning brighter than any sunset.

FROM TOP TO BOTTOM: They threw themselves over the edge; Faline was standing at one end of the island; Coming slowly across the river were the Great Prince and Bambi; There were no words for what Bambi was feeling. OPPOSITE: Sizzling embers flew through the air *(top)*; The current was stronger here and it swept them along *(bottom)*.

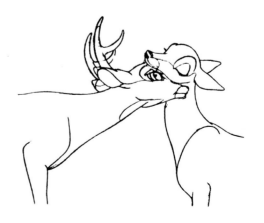

SPRING RETURNS

Even the blackened ruins of the forest held no power against spring. Another winter had ended, and now May's beautifying hand was passing lovingly across the charred landscape. Flowers were blooming everywhere. New leaves had sprouted from wounded branches, and a velvety coating of new spring grass was covering the scarred forest floor.

The old owl's favorite tree had managed to escape the worst of the fire. He was dozing there peacefully one morning when Thumper and his four children dashed up to a fallen log under the tree.

All four of them began drumming loudly and shouting up at the owl. "Wake up! Wake up, Friend Owl!" called Thumper excitedly. "Wake up, Friend Owl!" echoed the little rabbits.

New spring grass was covering the scarred forest floor (*above*); "Wake up, Friend Owl!" (*below*). OPPOSITE: The old owl's tree had escaped the worst of the fire. OVERLEAF: The blackened ruins of the forest held no power against spring.

The owl let out a little wail. "Oh, what *now?*" he said irritably, blinking down at the rabbits.

"It's happened! It's happened!" cried Thumper. Before the owl could ask any questions, the rabbits had dashed away.

Next Flower came scurrying past. "In the thicket!" he explained to the mystified owl. "Come on, Bambi!" he then called out over his shoulder.

"Yes, Papa, I'm coming," came a tiny voice behind him—and a baby skunk waddled along after his father.

Now that the Owl looked around, he could see that everyone in the forest seemed to be hurrying toward the thicket. Even the moles were tunneling along faster than usual, and Mrs. Quail's new line of chicks could hardly keep up with her.

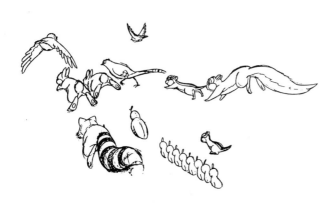

"Guess I'd better go see what's up," the owl grumbled. "Nobody ever takes the time to tell *me* anything."

Still complaining under his breath, he launched himself into the sweet-smelling air.

"Come on, Bambi!" called Flower. "Yes, Papa, I'm coming," said the baby skunk behind him *(top)*; Everyone in the forest seemed to be hurrying toward the thicket *(middle and bottom)*.

Faline was lying down in the thicket when the owl got there. Curled up next to her, staring wonderingly at the animals pressed around the thicket, was a tiny, perfect fawn.

"The spitting image of his father at that age," said the owl. "Congratula . . ."

Suddenly he broke off. At the sound of his voice, a second fawn's head had popped up from behind her brother. She gazed at the owl in amazement, then gave him a shy smile.

"Two of them!" gasped Mrs. Raccoon.

The old owl chuckled. "Yes, sir! I don't think I've ever seen a more likely-looking pair of fawns," he told Faline, who smiled graciously. "Prince Bambi must be mighty proud."

A nd he was. Bambi was standing guard on a cliff high above the thicket, where he could take in everything at a single glance—the thicket with his new family inside, the adoring circle of animals who were his friends, the forest springing into new life, and beyond, the wide green meadow.

As he gazed down over the scene, the Great Prince stood at his side. For a few minutes they watched the thicket together in silence. Slowly the old stag turned his serene gaze to Bambi, as if in farewell. Then without looking back, the Great Prince turned and walked away, leaving Bambi alone on the cliff.

Bambi's heart was full. Sadness at the old stag's passing mingled with joy at the birth of his children and his love for Faline. He straightened his shoulders and lifted his head proudly. In the golden sun, he was a majestic figure indeed, the new Prince of the Forest.

In the golden sun, he was a majestic figure indeed *(top);* "I don't think I've ever seen a more likely-looking pair of fawns," chuckled the old owl. "Prince Bambi must be mighty proud." *(above).*

THE FILM

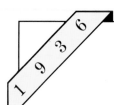
The Beginning

It's a story that's going to have a tremendous amount of appeal.

— WALT DISNEY

From the start, *Bambi* was a very different picture. It had a fantasy and reality all its own, separate from Walt Disney's other films. This was no imaginary forest that one could enter and leave at will. Whoever ventured in became part of an experience so strong that neither heart nor mind could ever forget its impact.

Snow White and the Seven Dwarfs is pure fairy tale and *Pinocchio* is a story of dreams come true. Only in *Bambi* do the tears linger. In spite of humor, beauty, and charm, even a lifetime does not diminish the memory of the shot that killed Bambi's mother and the anguish felt for the lonely little deer. Love's First Kiss or the wave of a Blue Fairy's wand could not undo this terrible moment. Its reality and truth were the story's strength and the prime ingredient in making *Bambi* such a different picture.

The Viennese author Felix Salten had gone even further in his original book *Bambi,* published in English in 1928. In addition to Man the hunter, he told of the many predators in the forest who killed daily for their own survival, but this was accepted as a natural occurrence because Salten's writing was so penetrating and his feelings so deep. Salten wrote of a young buck who believed Man was his friend, only to be betrayed; of the last two leaves

Even Walt Disney, genius of entertainment and storytelling, spent time with the live fawns, Bambi and Faline, who would help ground Bambi *in reality.*

on a tree contemplating death and the hereafter before the chill wind sent them swirling to the ground; of the dignity with which all the animals faced their uncertain futures. Instead of a story, however, it was a collection of incidents that enabled the young fawn Bambi to learn the profound lessons which in time made him the wisest deer in the forest. This was not a dramatic plot filled with passions and actions as much as a mosaic of isolated adventures, and as most producers said, quite impossible to make into a movie.

One of those who wanted to try was Sidney Franklin, outstanding live action director at MGM Studios. His own films were marked by a great understanding of the characters in a story, coupled with vast amounts of heart, romantic ideas, and most of all, sincerity. He bought the rights to the book in 1933 and started at once to find a way to bring it to the screen.

He searched for the right voices, recording Margaret Sullavan and Victor Jory as the two last leaves and testing several other outstanding actors for the voice of the Old Prince, but the performances were never quite as persuasive or believable as the written words. Sidney Franklin realized that the spirit of the book could never be captured that way.

The films from the Walt Disney Studio at that time were mainly built on gags and entertaining situations developed for Mickey, Donald, Pluto, and Goofy. The musical scores were tuneful and toe-tapping but relied more on a strong beat than any depth of expression. The *Silly Symphonies* had shown richness of character and even achieved a touch of pathos now and then, but the stories were simplistic and lighthearted. Still, animation itself offered a special magic, creating audience involvement through characters that existed nowhere other than in the imagination. If *Bambi* could not be made in live action the way Sidney Franklin thought it should be, perhaps the Disney Studio would have the necessary capabilities. In 1935, just as we were making the first experimental drawings on *Snow White,* Sidney Franklin contacted Walt to see if he was at all interested.

Sidney Franklin, director and producer of live-action films, including Private Lives, Goodbye Mr. Chips, *and* Mrs. Miniver, *hoped that Disney Studio's animation could bring* Bambi *to life.*

Walt was not only interested, he was thrilled, but by very different possibilities. He had no intention of making a film about realistic deer living in a forest. What Walt saw were personalities. As he said, "When I read the book, I got excited about the possibilities with animals, what we could do with them, not with doing the book the way it was." Where Sidney Franklin saw poetry, beauty, philosophy—the wind brushing softly against the tall grasses, the warm sun on the meadow, the grandeur of the forest and the majesty of the creatures who lived and died there—Walt Disney saw an entertaining cast that would give him an opportunity to fully utilize the talents of his staff, as well as his own, in

giving life and character traits to everything that lived in this forest.

No one will ever know just what influence Sidney Franklin had in helping Walt see a larger, grander, more emotional picture than he was considering. Walt was always ready to try something completely new if the idea intrigued him enough. Although he claimed that his main interest was in the animals' personalities, he found himself moved by many of the themes in the book, several of which would keep haunting him over the next few years. But at this time, while he thought he knew the special feeling he wanted in *Bambi,* he did not know how to achieve it, or even if it could be done.

None of us were ever completely confident that we would create such a truly emotional experience for the audience. The basic story of forest creatures living in idyllic surroundings, yet under the

Sidney Franklin and later artist Tyrus Wong saw the poetry, beauty, and philosophy in the grandeur of the forest and the meadow and the majesty of the creatures who lived there.

constant threat of death, provided scant material for our simple animation to convince the viewers of the reality of such dangers. One thing Walt realized quite early was that Man killing Bambi's mother would be the most powerful and memorable statement ever made in an animated film. No longer philosophical or an important lesson about survival, it spoke directly to the heart.

Embarking on a venture of this magnitude took an unusual amount of courage. How could we animate the scenes described in the book? When we read "Bambi looked at him, filled with a wonderful ecstasy, and shaken by a mysterious tremor," we found nothing we could draw. Inner feelings were beyond our abilities at that time—far beyond; yet Walt seemed resolved to go ahead. He had learned how to achieve mood, effects, color, and audience communication in his short films, so possibly he saw no problem in creating wonderful ecstasy and mysterious tremors in animation. We wondered if he was really aware of how much of a challenge he was facing.

Walt's first feature film, *Snow White and the Seven Dwarfs,* continued to demand all of his time and energy, as he was determined to make this first feature film better than most of his live action competition. It was December of 1936 before he could concentrate on *Bambi* and April of 1937 before the contracts were set and the rights to the story turned over to him. Sidney Franklin was engaged to collaborate on the film for a period of three and a half years. It was another five years before *Bambi* was finally completed, but friendship prevailed beyond the limits of the contract.

Walt had always been far ahead of his staff in his dreams and plans for the studio. This had usually been a source of stimulation and a challenge as we tried to bring his unusual ideas to the screen. But when we heard that he had decided *Bambi* should be our second feature just as we were beginning animation on *Snow White,* we felt he had made a serious error.

"We're not even sure *Snow White* will go over — what's he doing planning a second feature already?"

"There's no story there for an animated film."

"It's not a story at all."

"Did you hear that record of the two leaves talking? We can't do that."

"Who can animate deer?"

The many and varied research paintings and drawings explored ways to capture the moods and emotions expressed in Felix Salten's book, providing the foundation for their realization in animation.

Bambi *provided an opportunity to create more of the captivating, believable, animated characters that had been a large part of the innovative success of* Snow White and the Seven Dwarfs.

Types and Characters

Everybody in life can be funny. We all have funny little ways. . . . I don't think you should call them comics. You should think of them as types and characters.

— WALT DISNEY

Early in 1937 Walt chose Perce Pearce and Larry Morey as the two men to head up his story crew for *Bambi*. Both had proven themselves invaluable during the creation of *Snow White*'s dwarfs, building them into seven distinct personalities, and he felt they would bring the same sympathetic approach to *Bambi*.

Next to Walt, Perce was the best storyteller and actor; he knew how to characterize the specific traits of an individual. He loved to get up and perform for us and even became identified with many of the cartoon cast on each picture. Larry had written the lyrics for Frank Churchill's marvelous tunes in *Snow White*. His work was outstanding because his words were not only simple and expressive, but had a way of advancing the story while helping the audience get acquainted with the penciled performers. Together Perce and Larry made a unique team that would give *Bambi* a consistent look of quality considerably above that of our recent happy little cartoons.

Dave Hand was in charge of all production at the studio. He had come up through the ranks of animation and was the supervising director of *Snow White*. Dave understood the complexities that faced animators on feature productions and

Walt believed that especially rich characters would lead to a story line and provide the necessary entertainment.

ABOVE: Frank Churchill (left), Ed Plumb (middle), and Larry Morey (right) created the wonderful songs and music in Bambi. LEFT: Along with Larry Morey, Dave Hand (left) and Perce Pearce (right) were the first men assigned to Bambi.

insisted that each story point, each scene, each gag be clear and solid. He once told us, "I'm not as creative as some of you, but I can make it work better than most of you." He was right.

To these three men Walt outlined his feelings about this new picture, asking especially for rich personalities in the animals that would then lead to some kind of story line. There should be more humor in the picture than in the book, and that would probably come from additional interesting creatures. His final instructions were, as usual, "We will have to . . . get hold of our characters before we can build the story."

He felt there were good possibilities in a sequence with the animals discussing Man. "The dramatic part comes when they see Man and are scared and run. Then they talk about it very seriously, but the humor comes from the fact they are talking about us—about the way we appear to them. . . . That sequence should be comic. In the book it is too serious." He felt this could be one of the highlights of the picture.

Walt liked the ideas about the skunk, who was slightly belligerent and could make anybody back down. If an argument starts, he asks, "You want to make something out of it?" The other fellow quickly says, "No, Sir." Another favorite was the gentlemanly Mr. Hare, well-mannered philosopher and storyteller, who had to constantly run from the fox. The hare was respected in the forest neighborhood and there was an opportunity for considerable pathos in his role.

It was a beginning, but a very mild beginning. The staff looked hopefully to Walt, but he was not giving his usual strong leadership this time. The storymen reported that he seemed troubled by the whole idea of the picture and was not sure of which way to go. The story elements were extremely elusive and the problems of a convincing presentation were enormous. Even *Snow White* was continuing to cause Walt and his crew problems because they had not yet realized that the basic story was a murder mystery. An evil monarch was trying to kill an innocent girl. *Bambi* had much the same structure; evil Man was trying to kill the innocent deer in the forest. And that was an impossible premise for an animated film in 1937.

Snow White would not be released for another six months, and while it looked promising, even exciting, we were not sure that an audience would take it seriously. Would they boo the witch? Would they accept the dwarfs crying around Snow White's bier? Would an audience sit still for an animated film that lasted well over an hour? We were sure of the gags and the entertainment we had created, but the success of a whole feature

In early meetings, Mr. Hare was an important figure, the head of a large family, and well-respected in the forest community.

film was as yet untried. What could we count on for *Bambi?*

During a meeting in September, Perce asked Walt if he still wanted *Bambi* for the Christmas release in 1938 as originally planned. Walt answered, "We should strive for it. It would be ideal to come out with a feature every year." But afterwards he did some hard thinking. *Bambi* was not far enough along even to require a full story crew. By this time, most of the story department had begun working on *Pinocchio*. It was more like the best of the *Silly Symphonies,* only longer, and seemed to be devoid of these unsettling problems Walt was encountering on *Bambi*. As a leading storyman said, "*Pinocchio* was a picture Walt knew how to make, while *Bambi* still baffled him." The decision was made to move the story of the wooden puppet ahead of *Bambi* on the schedule.

Walt began spending more time in meetings on *Bambi* and finally, once again, the ideas started flowing. Equally important, Walt was enjoying the process of building entertaining material. Soon the cast included a weasel, a mole, a possum, and an excitable spider who yelled at Bambi, "Watch out! You're tearing my web to pieces. A whole day's work gone." The skunk was becoming more important: there was a suggestion that he should talk about the awful scent of Man. Ants, jaybirds, raccoons, beavers, and the owl began to emerge, along with a comedy team of a squirrel and chipmunk.

Walt said of raccoons, "A raccoon is always washing its food. It washes everything it eats. I saw that animal as a kind of nut . . . the type that wipes off the knife and fork and [is] always wiping out a cup before he pours his tea."

Walt immediately liked the character of a belligerent skunk (above, left); An early story idea had Bambi swallow a bee and other creatures shout evacuation instructions to it through his ear (above).

This turned out to be a very fortunate move for both the studio and the picture, for none of us knew enough at that time to make a film of the *Bambi* story or were even aware of how much more could be done with the animation medium. We were in a period of great growth that would bring advancements in our skills and a new knowledge of how to build feelings in the audience's imagination. The animators were becoming actors and the rest of the staff were learning how to be filmmakers, leaving the quaint characters and the pretty scenes of the *Silly Symphonies* behind.

Popular as those short subjects were, if we had gone ahead with *Bambi* as planned, it surely would have been a failure. There would have been funny gags on the incidental characters but no humor in the story itself. The death of the mother would have been one of the incidents, certainly, but without a convincing buildup, without the strong attachment between mother and son, without the concern of the audience, it would have meant little. How could we capture the warmth and appeal that would make the audience care? We all needed more experience.

A favorite episode involved an ill-tempered bee whom Bambi met on the meadow. He warns the young deer, "Watch where you're eating," but soon Bambi is saying to the squirrel and chipmunk, "I think I swallowed the bee." Sure enough there is buzzing coming from Bambi's stomach, along with muffled yelling. The squirrel asks Bambi to open his mouth so they can hear what the bee is

saying and they are blasted with *"Get me out of here!"* The squirrel and chipmunk run to Bambi's ear to shout suggestions to the bee, then back to his mouth for the answers. The whole disturbance gives Bambi a bad case of hiccups which increases his guest's discomfort considerably. The squirrel calls to Bambi to drink some water to end the hiccups, but the bee yells back, "No, no, I can't swim." When the bee is finally dislodged, he comes shooting out of Bambi's mouth, buzzing fitfully, with a violent case of hiccups of his own.

Walt commented, "I like the screwball attitude with the characters. It keeps them from being straight. I like that situation because I can visualize it with the sound effects of the bee in Bambi's stomach. I think we are getting something that is not just the old type of gag."

In addition to the humor, there were other aspects of the film which Walt wanted to see developed. He was beginning to see more beauty in the forest surroundings. He had always liked the idea of a lullaby, probably sung by Bambi's mother, but now he thought the wind might have a voice and be able to sing. He described how he saw Bambi walking with his mother to the meadow, she progressing carefully while he stops to look at things, then half runs to keep up.

I see a pretty sunrise scene, with a silhouette of the two deer. From that we would gradually merge into where they are going: through thickets, along paths, into where the sun can streak in a little, where they would go into shadow, and where you would see

Early characters included a squirrel-and-chipmunk comedy duo; Ken Hultgren drew these squirrel character suggestions (above); Walt described the beauty he envisioned as Bambi and his mother moved through the forest (below).

nothing again but silhouette. You would hear the conversation going on all the time. He would be like a kid running behind his mother and asking questions.

After another month, Walt felt it was time to present to Sidney Franklin the work that had been done. He sent the script with this explanation: "This is our first draft of the story which covers the chapters from Bambi's birth through his first walk in the woods, bringing in the various animals he meets there. The dialogue and cutting is still very rough." After four years of waiting and dreaming, it was an exciting moment for Sidney Franklin. On October 20, he met with Walt and the *Bambi* crew.

It was important that a suggestion of the nobility of Bambi's character be presented early on and that he should be proven a hero, as when he fights off the dogs that are holding Faline captive.

Sidney Franklin's reactions reflected his great integrity and taste. Generally he thought that the storymen were getting too far away from Bambi in the incidents they were developing. Bambi should be the star and we should see the story and the other characters through his eyes. He felt they should build into the story very early a suggestion of the nobility of Bambi's character, to show his kindness as well as his inquisitiveness, and should also build in a little more feeling of motherly love on the part of Bambi's mother. He did not like the bee sequence, being bothered by the fact that the bee was inside the fawn.

Sidney Franklin saw a larger role for Mr. Hare, having him stop to tell Bambi a story each time he meets him but running out of the scene as the fox comes after him. He is always telling the same story and he never gets to finish it.

In the chase, near the end of the picture, where the hunt is going on, the hare will be shot. Bambi stops and asks him if he is all right. The hare, who knows he is going to die, and Bambi, who also realizes the hare won't live, have a scene together. Bambi tells the hare he never really heard the end of the story. The hare wants to tell Bambi the story. We hear the hunt approaching and shots being fired offstage, but in spite of the danger that Bambi is in, he stands there listening. The hare gets part way into the story when he dies. As he dies, he might say something like this: IT WASN'T A VERY FUNNY STORY ANYWAY. THERE WAS NO POINT TO IT. . . . Bambi would stand there looking at the hare for a moment. We might see tears gather in Bambi's eyes. Offstage we hear several shots quite close to Bambi. As the men come on, Bambi leaps with a mighty jump over something, and leaves.

This type of scene had been used in many excellent MGM live action films and it might have worked in *Bambi* as well. It probably could have been animated, even with such subtle acting and so much dialogue, but mainly it showed us a new dimension that was possible for animation: real drama with the communication of an idea that

Sidney Franklin's reactions to the first draft of the story script helped create a new dimension in both the research and animation: real drama and the communication of an idea that would move the audience.

would move the audience. It was a sobering thought and a provocative challenge.

Walt liked much of what he heard and appreciated the reasons for the suggestions. He probably realized that up to this time he had been adapting slightly more subtle versions of the same kinds of gags that were used in the shorts, but something more was needed here. A full story, especially this story, was not the same as the fairy tales that had been Walt's specialty. He was now discovering another type of picture, one that would represent his own development of the ideas in the book.

New dialogue was written, gags were cut, and the script was revised. On December 15, they all met again. This time Sidney Franklin was pleased. "You have hit the spirit of the story with this. This is *Bambi*. There is no gag that stands out above Bambi, himself. He is part of everything."

Walt felt that they did not portray enough of the menace of the forest. "It should be done with action," Sidney Franklin responded, "not with words. You must develop that feeling of danger. . . . It should be done with business and not by talking about it so much." Felix Salten had written a dramatic scene of a single dog who chased the fox to exhaustion, then killed him. In Walt's mind, the lone dog became a whole swarm of hunting dogs snarling and lunging after Faline, Bambi's mate.

> While the hunt is going on, and the smaller animals are being shot here and there, Faline and Bambi become separated. The hounds follow Faline, baying for the hunters, and Bambi tries to locate Faline. All this time, the hunters are coming closer and closer. The dogs finally have Faline at bay, and you don't know who is going to reach her first, the hunters or Bambi. Bambi rushes in and attacks the dogs, tossing them in the brush, and scaring them away. Bambi and Faline run away just as the hunters come up, and as the two deer run over the hill, the hunters shoot after them, fraying the brush all around them. . . . I would like to see Bambi as the hero, even if he has to be wounded to prove it.

Walt continued, exploring the potential for drama. "I think the audience expects to see the fantasy in this. . . . There is a chance for some beautiful stuff with these changing seasons. I would like to see, during the winter sequence, a little musical sequence with the crystal formations of snow. We could get some beautiful shapes of trees covered with snow, the sun streaming through, and the snow falling off. Then after Bambi's mother is shot, the blizzard comes up, and he is all alone in the worst part of the winter." And further, "I see a marvelous scene after the forest fire. We will fade out on the fire, and fade in on the following morning, with all the charred tree trunks silhouetted like crosses against the morning sky. It is a very desolate scene—devastated. We see the silhouettes of Bambi and the Old Stag coming through the fog and smoke. The Stag brings Bambi to the place where Man is, then leaves him. We see the Stag going over the hill, and Bambi left alone."

Felix Salten had ended his story with an old and wise Bambi chastising two fawns who were crying for their mother. Mr. Franklin had a new idea. "I think it would be beautiful here if, instead of just having Bambi meet the two little deer walking in the forest, we repeated the circumstances of Bambi's own birth. You can get a magnificent effect with the wind and the same choral effect used in the opening episode. Then come up to a long shot of Bambi standing on the hill alone, a full-screen silhouette."

WALT: I think this ending is much stronger. . . . This completes the cycle.

SIDNEY FRANKLIN: Having him meet the two young deer is a charming picture, but it doesn't have the dramatic effect. The audience loves to feel they have seen a cycle completed, and that they have seen the whole life of a character.

The stirring visuals that Walt sought in the changing seasons were first explored in research art, such as this painting by Harold Miles, and later in animation.

119

WALT: Before this last episode, I would like to see a montage—the deer going away, winter, snow and sleet falling on the burned forest, building up to an effect of nothing but snow. Then come back upon the next spring, with the snow melting and everything turning green. . . . After seeing everything burned, we want to see it come back to life in the same happy way.

Together these two unusual men had found an approach to satisfy both of them and had kindled confidence that a film could be made of *Bambi* after all. Walt had come a long way from those early meetings when he felt more comfortable with squirrels and bees than he did with deer and Man. Now his ideas were about structure, continuity, and the beauty and drama to be found in this tale of the forest.

For all their agreement, however, neither addressed the basic problem still confronting them: how could deer be made into the enthralling actors who would be the charismatic stars of a feature film? For it would take more than engaging personalities, bits of comedy, warm relationships, and drama to make a successful film of *Bambi*. But the picture was definitely on its way. There was a beginning and an ending, with an exciting climax and dramatic heart tug in the middle.

Nineteen thirty-seven ended on an exceptionally high note for the studio. *Snow White and the Seven Dwarfs* was released on December 21 and became an immediate success. In one glorious night the animated cartoon jumped from the lowest spot on a movie program to the best-loved film of the year. As we bought every review, every magazine, every newspaper that carried any kind of story about the studio, we felt that we could lick any problem, animate any action, make any story into a great film. Nineteen thirty-eight would be our year!

Both Walt and Sidney Franklin agreed that the picture should end with a majestic shot of Bambi standing alone on top of a hill. OPPOSITE: *After the forest fire, there could be a great dramatic moment showing the charred remains of the trees standing like crosses in a graveyard.*

Drawing from Nature

We have them talking and the minute you have them say a word, you've got that human parallel established, so I mean in their mannerisms—in their action—it should all be based on certain human things.

— WALT DISNEY

Snow White and the *Seven Dwarfs* was the studio's greatest achievement, especially sweet after the criticism from the Hollywood experts who had dubbed it "Disney's Folly." Walt paid off his loans, began hiring more employees, expanded his thinking for both *Pinocchio* and *Bambi* and bought the land for the fabulous studio he would build out in Burbank, the one designed specifically for animation.

Up to this time, *Bambi* had consisted of dreams, thoughts, outlines, and a great deal of talk. Now drawings, research, film, photographs, and lengthy notes began to fill each room at the studio. Artist and photographer Maurice ("Jake") Day sent photographs of his Maine woods in summer, fall, winter, and spring, not missing Indian summer; in rain, heavy snow, light snow, and sleet; on gray days and on bright, sparkling days— every bit of nature's variety. He even arranged to have two fawns shipped out to the studio in June so the artists would have live models to study. A pen was built alongside the building where the deer, christened Bambi and Faline, could be ob-

In addition to humor through characters, Walt wanted to develop more of the beauty in the forest surroundings.

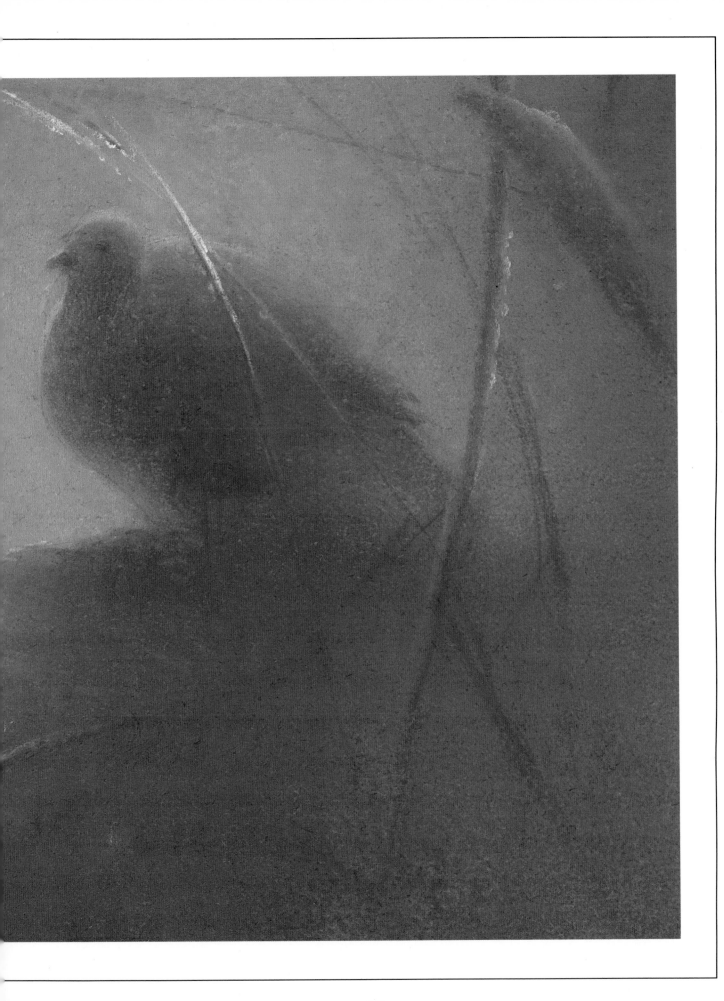

Carl Fallberg headed his own story unit on Bambi *and made special friends with the live Faline.*

served at all times of day or evening by simply looking out the window. Other animals were brought in and almost overnight, the unit had its own zoo.

The artists drew from these photographs and live models, from film, from trips to the Los Angeles Zoo, from memory, and from imagination. Their teacher was Bernard Garbutt, who organized field trips, lectured, gave drawing lessons, and taught them about the real animal world. "Garby" was the animal expert; he could draw any animal, at any age, in any position, and he set the standard for everyone else to follow. An outstanding naturalist—almost more so than an artist—he knew the actions of the animals and the relative positions of each (the relationship of the head to the neck, the neck to the shoulders, the shoulders to the back, etc.) in any given actions, but he had

little feeling for animation. There were no thrusts or strength of movement in his drawings, no sense of inner life, and nothing of the animal's feelings. He believed the story of *Bambi* called for realistic drawings and that there should be absolutely no humanizing of the deer in the picture. This seemed to be what everyone expected for *Bambi,* so for many months the kind and gentle Garby was the undisputed master.

The direction changed, however, with the arrival of Marc Fraser Davis. Marc's own art training had been sporadic, but he had maintained a keen interest in drawing animals. In San Francisco he had studied art in the mornings and then taken the trolley out to the Fleischacker Zoo to draw real animals. More hours were spent at the library studying comparative animal anatomy. Marc sensed innately that there was more to drawing an

Bernard Garbutt's realistic drawings caught the essence of the animal, but lacked fluid animation (above), *whereas Marc Davis brought life and feeling to his drawings, which became guides for all to follow* (right).

animal than a meticulous outline of its external features. Its thoughts were as important as how it moved and both were inherent in its basic design.

At the Disney Studio, Marc was better prepared than most to draw deer that could be animated. He looked for ways to make the whole figure show personality, acting, and attitudes that were distinctly human. His deer looked like deer, for they had lost none of their essential animal appearance or character, but they could be understood as having human thoughts and feelings. Faline was coy, she was spirited and playful, she had a twinkle in her eye; she sparkled. Through Marc's work, even the skeptics saw the possibility of a picture with deer as sympathetic main characters—that is, if the animators could do as well in their turn. It was the first major breakthrough on this very special picture.

In Marc Davis's drawings of Faline, even the skeptics saw the possibilities of deer as sympathetic main characters.

Clair Weeks, artist and story sketch man, said, "It was . . . sort of a little paradise we had . . . free of the hurly-burly of Hyperion—nobody bothered us." No one made trips back to the main studio and the only person who came over to Seward was Mr. Keener, the paymaster.

Work on the story progressed slowly and carefully as small story units searched for ideas and situations that would hold an audience's interest simply through the play of personalities in a wonderful setting. One of the few storymen who also did his own story sketches was Mel Shaw, a true natural artist who was particularly sensitive to the visual possibilities in the surroundings as well as to the appealing actions of the characters. At a meeting with Perce and Larry, Mel presented his ideas on Bambi and his mother's first walk near their thicket by de-

The expansion that followed *Snow White*'s success soon had the studio on Hyperion Avenue overcrowded and spilling into nearby apartment buildings and vacant office space, wherever it could be found. Farthest away was an old film studio on Seward Street in Hollywood which became home for the *Bambi* unit for over a year. The deer had to be left behind, but the animators who were preparing themselves to work on *Bambi*—but who had not yet been assigned to Seward Street—took the opportunity to get to know the live Bambi and Faline.

At first there was much resentment over on Seward at being separated from the stimulation of the main studio, but gradually the staff realized that there were certain benefits in being isolated.

Animal expert Bernard Garbutt gave lectures on anatomy and realistic drawing to the Bambi *artists and here shows a baby alligator to Marc Davis* (left), *Retta Scott* (middle), *and Mel Shaw* (right).

Jim Algar was the director for the first half of Bambi, *having trained as an animator on* Snow White *and directed "The Sorcerer's Apprentice" in* Fantasia.

scribing this continuity: "Opening on a semi-dark forest with the sunbeams coming through, and Bambi and his mother just step into the light. . . . They walk along and you can hear the wind humming through the leaves. . . . There would be something very mysterious about it."

Larry immediately suggested a musical theme for the wind. But while the feelings for the magic of the forest and the voice in the wind had charm and beauty, they had very little solid audience entertainment as yet. The three then considered a voice in the gurgling of the brook, a change of sound when Bambi put his foot in the water, a reflection, and the possibility of his inadvertently getting his nose in the water and the startled reaction that would follow.

This led to a scene with the owl and the start of a light shower. The first drops hit the owl in the eye, causing him to back up; the squirrel and chipmunk go into their hole in the tree; a mother bird flies to her nest and spreads her wings over her babies to protect them from the rain. Perce suggested they show "the rabbit family moving under the roots—and all those little eyes." Mel wondered if they weren't making too big a buildup for a spring shower and Perce agreed, "It seems like you're preparing for a storm."

As they talked, a storm sounded like a better idea, and they discussed thunderclaps and a song

for the raindrops reminiscent of a round, with repeating words, "I like falling, I like falling." Larry remembered one of the photos Jake Day had sent from Maine. "If we could get the effect like in Jake's picture of the raindrops on the leaves and then the sun comes out on the foliage there, it would make a very beautiful shot to end on." Perce agreed that the song should have a very special ending, a visual image to remember. Larry continued, "Supposing it stopped raining before the end of our song. I LIKE FALLING—I LIKE FALLING. And it stops raining and the sun comes out and then just the dripping of water off the leaves makes I LIKE— I LIKE—I——I———."

Most of what they talked about remained in that sequence, enhanced with additional story ideas and startling effects animation. The storm became a very real thunderstorm with lightning flashes and driving rain, brief but exciting. *Bambi* was starting to take shape.

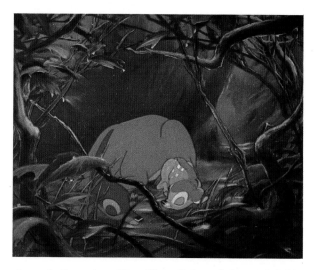

An early discussion of Bambi's walk through the woods led to the development of the thunderstorm sequence and the use of music to mimic the falling raindrops that at first keep Bambi from his sleep and then provide a lullaby. OVERLEAF: *Sketches such as this gave way to more complete drawings.*

B.6

Sc.4

8EQ.07.0

F-2002

.04

(GLASS PLATEN CEL)

0.4-B

0.4-B
LEAVES

B6. #2

B6. #3

(.05) CEL
POPPIES

.04 (BOT PEG CEL)

.03 (GLASS)

(GLASS)

.02 (SKY)
PAPER
MASONITE

U4B

BOTTOM
PEGS

(MOVES AT
.04)

6½ F-2P4N
CELL

.00 | .00

LEFT EDGE
OF GLASS
B.C #1

2

B6 #1

6½ F-20" G
MOVES AT .03

CENT
START
6C #1

ENLARGE TO 12½" TOL 1/16

POS IF RT HAND
TREE ON U-4B

CENT
STOP
RIG #1

U-4B START

U-4B STOP

raddually the scattered individual sketches were changing into related drawings that told a story and expressed the inner feelings of the characters. Almost forgotten were the two fawns from Maine who still resided in the pen back at Hyperion. One dark and misty morning in mid-October, a wild young buck came down from the hills to visit Faline. We knew that deer lived over in Griffith Park near the Hollywood hills, but that was over a mile away and across two busy thoroughfares. From our work, we had come to think of our fawns as something akin to cartoon animals, gentle, kindly, cute, and playful—certainly never ruled by any instinctual drives. Here, we were unexpectedly face-to-face with the very Nature we had been drawing so casually.

As we approached, the visitor lowered his head with its young, sharp antlers and looked at us defiantly. He was strong and intense and bursting with that inner life that most of us had failed to capture in our drawings. We moved back. Cars raced along Hyperion Avenue and curious people gathered to watch this real-life drama being played out on the grounds of the world's greatest make-believe kingdom. The buck became apprehensive and pranced nervously about on the slippery asphalt of the street. The SPCA had been called, but the situation was rapidly becoming threatening for everyone. The buck's head was raised in near panic and his eyes bulged as he darted back and forth, trying to find a way out of the crowd.

At that moment, Assistant Director Larry Lansburgh, who had once been a rodeo stunt rider, stepped out of the studio with a lariat in his hand. As the buck bolted across a vacant lot, a carefully thrown loop from Larry's lasso settled around his neck, halting his flight. Quickly, Larry had him down and hogtied, rodeo style, before the buck could hurt himself or any of the spectators. It was a dazzling moment of high energy and left us too stunned to move. Larry kept the buck under control until the SPCA crew arrived while we studied the defiant animal, impressed by his intensity and vitality. Faline looked wistfully after him in the departing truck and the rest of us returned to the studio with a new understanding of the animals we were trying to draw.

TOP: *Bernard Garbutt's expertise in naturalistic drawing gave* Bambi *artists the framework in which to work magic.*
ABOVE: *Bambi and Faline receive visiting music consultants* (from left to right) *Leopold Stokowski and Deems Taylor, along with Walt.*

During this time, Walt was learning much about music and its potential as a powerful part of any motion picture. Every afternoon at four o'clock he met with conductor Leopold Stokowski and music critic and composer Deems Taylor to discuss well-known classical pieces that might fit into an animated concert feature—*Fantasia*—and to learn more about the history of the selections and any anecdotes about the composers.

The English illustrator David Hall captured in realistic detail the momentum and emotion of the charge from the meadow.

Art Director Tom Codrick (above, left) *guided the extraordinary group of painters and illustrators, including Maurice Noble, Gustaf Tenggren, David Hall, Harold Miles,*

Travis Johnson, Charles Paysant, Zack Schwartz, Lew Keller, John Arensma, Stan Spohn, Jules Engel, and Dick Anthony (above, right).

This was all new to Walt. In the early days he had used "mood music" to fortify the thrills and chases and happy dances in the *Silly Symphonies,* but it had always been performed by a small group of musicians that could not create a strong orchestral effect. Walt's successes had been with laughs and he was skeptical of too much seriousness in any project. As he approached *Bambi,* he followed his proven procedure. He asked Frank Churchill to write more songs like those he had written for *Snow White.* Soon there were melodies and thematic material for the little stream, the raindrops, and the two winds, all light and cheerful. These would work well with the gags and personalities that were developing in the story.

On *Fantasia,* however, Walt was learning more about music and how it could create mental images and manipulate the listener in subtle, psychological ways. Walt discovered that he was very susceptible to the powers of music; he could scarcely

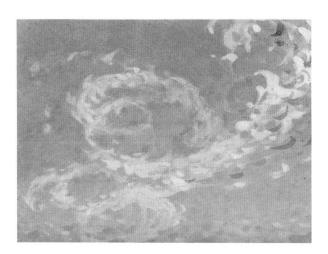

These artists produced atmosphere sketches for Bambi *as beautiful as any impressionist paintings.*

Harold Miles worked as a conceptual artist under Tom Codrick creating works such as this evocative painting of deer deep in a forest glade (above); *The story line was still uncertain, but the drawings were of top quality* (below).

believe what was happening the day he found himself whistling a Beethoven theme as he walked down the hall. He was also beginning to realize the exciting potential in the music for *Bambi* but as yet could find no time to start work on it.

Perce continued to move things along, with his own kind of perfection. The story was still uncertain, but the drawings were of top quality, with the most beautiful and complete story sketches ever seen. On other films, story sketches depicted action and expressions with very little suggestion of the background or anything else. On *Bambi*, the goal was to uncover every possible way of telling the story and staging it to fit the overall theme of beauty, intimacy, and grandeur. Each drawing was a work of art.

Perce was full of fun as well as perfection and

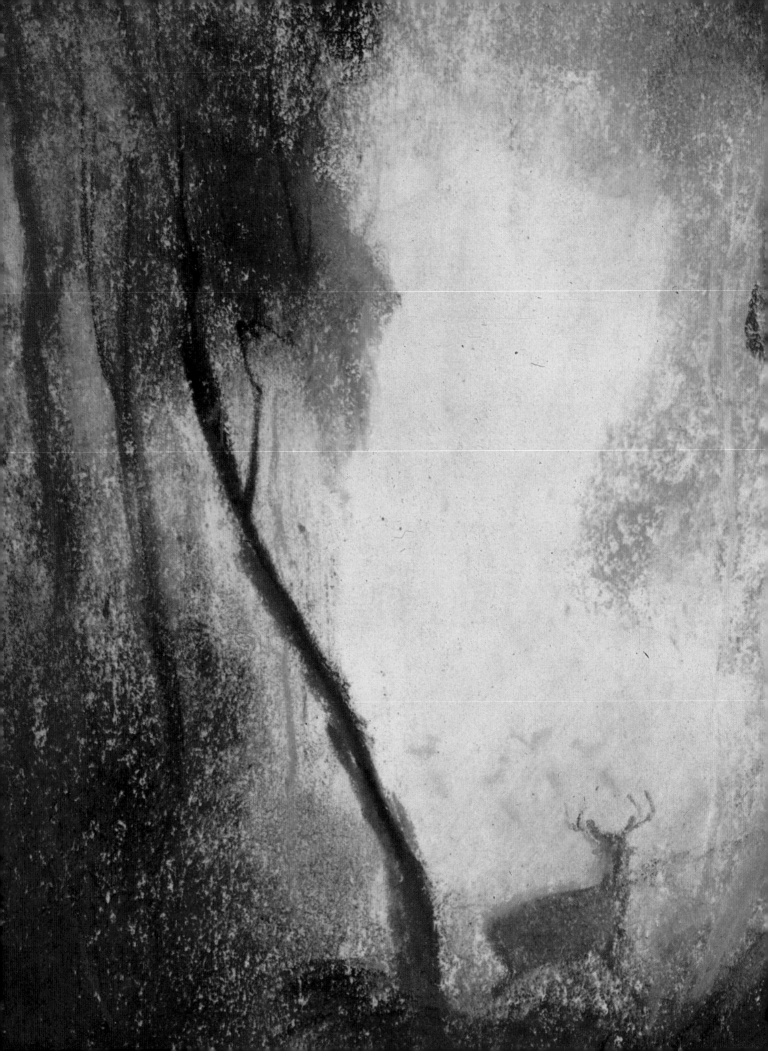

The goal was to uncover every possible way of telling the story and to stage it to fit the overall theme of beauty, intimacy, and grandeur (above and opposite).

loved to act out the roles of the animals in the film. In the morning, it was the owl. He would come into the building with a jolly hoot and a chuckle and the greeting, "Well hello, you critters—how's everybody on the meadow this morning?" Then he would "fluff his feathers" a few times and go off to his office. Later it might be the little mole who popped up out of his burrow at Bambi's feet, squinted at the bright sky overhead, and commented, "Nice, sunny day," then plunged back underground to continue on his way. In fact, Perce said this line so well, and so often, that he was talked into recording it for the film.

Perce's ad-lib acting and dialogue was good for the picture, because it kept the characters alive for the story crew. It was impossible to be around him for long without thinking of the *Bambi* cast as a group of friends one had known for a long time.

With the coming of winter, however, there was some restlessness at the Seward Street studio.

Walt had given the *Bambi* crew a long leash in the explorations of how to get the picture going, but as time wore on there was concern about where they were going and if they would ever get there. Would the picture ever be made? Would they ever get back to the mainstream of work at the studio or would they be forgotten? They made drawings of each other as personnel in the French Foreign Legion, isolated at a desert outpost.

But also by the end of the year, much progress had been made. Many voices for the characters had been selected, there were new scripts, and the sketches to illustrate them. The walls were covered with displays. There were paintings and drawings of the deep woods and stately forests, individual drawings of all the animals under consideration, model sheets, suggested layouts, backgrounds, and stacks of storyboards, all ready for Walt to see. But Walt never came. The feeling of isolation grew.

Breaking New Ground

I welcome the opportunity to break away from the traditional way of doing things. It is a picture that will stand it.

—WALT DISNEY

The "long leash" style of story research had led some of the artists to feel that, without Walt's guidance, Perce and Larry had been unable to make up their minds on the project. Others felt that the limitless possibilities of the assignment had kept everyone pursuing new ideas when they should have been consolidating what they had. Still others felt that amid the stacks of exploration were true gems that would not have come to light any other way. And throughout the year, more and more of these treasures were discovered, adding credence to their evaluation.

All of this had given Walt a chance to think longer about *Bambi*'s perplexing problems. He knew there were exceptional characters, strong drama, and a feeling of warmth in the *Bambi* film, but he was not sure we could get the audience involvement that was needed. The studio animators would soon be available for new assignments but Walt felt that *Bambi* should not be rushed into production. His heart was currently in exploring the use of classical music with animation. It was not difficult to change his mind about the schedule, and once again *Bambi* was moved back. *Fantasia* took its place as Disney's third animated feature.

Once all of the selections had been made for the music for *Fantasia*, Walt turned again to *Bambi*. He wanted to see what had been done with the

This production background painting by Robert McIntosh shows the influence of Tyrus Wong's style on the overall atmosphere of the film.

story and what use had been made of all the research and beautiful drawings and paintings. Moreover, rather than sitting through days of meetings, he wanted to see it all on film, as a story reel, running in sync with dialogue and sound effects. This meant selecting each drawing, photographing it in sequence on the animation camera, and correcting and editing as the film came back from the lab. It could not be done overnight. Neither Perce nor Larry had ever expected this kind of a showing; their instructions to explore had encouraged them to accumulate ideas that could best be presented one at a time in a conference.

It was clearly time for the supervising director, the practical and energetic Dave Hand, to move over to Seward Street. One storyman agreed, "If Dave hadn't got in there, Perce and Larry would still be on those storyboards." He was admired and respected by the men who liked to keep things progressing in their units and needed decisions every few days in order to move on. But Dave's robust style of making decisions was generally upsetting to any crew who had adjusted to a very relaxed way of working. The painters trying to find the right style for the picture or the perfect color scheme for a mood wished he would stay far, far away. They used to draw up petitions almost weekly requesting that Dave be taken off the picture. What did they do with them? "Oh, we always threw them away!"

By April, there were nearly twenty minutes of footage ready for viewing, but Perce did not want to run it for Walt until he had tested it first with some less crucial critics and had had a chance to correct any confusing sections. For this special screening he chose Don Graham, our art instructor, who had been lured from Chouinard's Art School five years earlier, and Rico Lebrun, probably the greatest draftsman of animals in the country. Rico Lebrun had been hired by Walt to help the eager, young crew of animators learn to draw four-footed creatures, both small and large. His knowledge was enormous, his taste and judgment impeccable, and his

While a horse never figured in Bambi, *art instructors Don Graham and Rico Lebrun believed comparative anatomy was important in understanding all animals and animal drawing.*

enthusiasm contagious. He loved the studio, but he really did not expect much from a collection of story sketches by Disney artists. What he saw amazed him: "You have talent here . . . fine artists on their own score."

Perce was pleased but quite concerned about the job facing the animators when they eventually would begin working on the picture.

PERCE: We are piling up a lot of reference material to influence many animators in the action, timing, and movement of real animals. We must capture a spirit of reality interpreted in fantasy. We must get poetry out of our pictorial side.

DON GRAHAM: I feel that fantasy and poetry are one and the same thing. Just the fact that you don't try to make funny-looking raindrops is good. You are absolutely right on this in your feeling. It's fantasy.

RICO LEBRUN: To what extent will you use reality?

PERCE: We can't just make them straight animals. We want to caricature animals as animals . . . not as though some human was dressed up in a deer suit. . . . What we have to try to do is make the audience feel, for the duration of the picture, that these are real animals.

RICO LEBRUN: You really have to go to nature. The little fawn is a pretty big handful in the sense of grace. It's all there. . . . The real thing has got it. What you have to do is make a poetical translation of it.

PERCE: Bambi's ability to convince you of his being a real animal is, I think, seventy-five percent dependent on the way he acts.

RICO LEBRUN: That's right. Bambi is an actor. He will create his own special world around him. . . . I think you have a tremendous problem on your hands.

Ty Wong brought his special touch to the animals as well as the backgrounds in the film; his graceful deer (above) *carries a certain resemblance to the more familiar figure* (below).

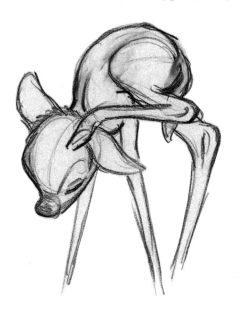

In a few more weeks the whole first third of the picture was ready to be shown to Walt and a special audience. In addition to storymen and directors, there were the three supervising animators who had been selected to work on this film—Milt Kahl, Frank Thomas, and Eric Larson. *Bambi* would be their responsibility for the next two years, and they were particularly eager to see the advance work on this production that had been kept so secret over on Seward Street.

The film contained most of the originally planned sequences: the babbling brook, a lengthy squirrel and chipmunk routine, and Bambi's mother taking her son around the neighborhood and teaching him to talk. Thumper was only a miscellaneous rabbit in a large family. Mr. and Mrs. Hare were the important members of this rabbit clan.

The young animals were extremely cute—almost excessively cute—and their bland actions and dialogue were too reminiscent of the early *Silly Symphonies*. But there was something else that worried us even more than that. "What kind of a cartoon is this? The mother gets shot!! You don't do that!" We animators saw too little entertainment and too much harsh drama. We were stunned.

The weaknesses in the story were summed up in the problems we found with the death of the mother. She had not been established as a sympathetic, caring character, and the dangers in the lives of the animals had not been made convincing. Her death seemed out of place because it was presented as just an unfortunate occurrence in the young fawn's life. It could take on meaning only if all of the ingredients in the film began to work together, both in terms of filmmaking and in the establishment of a forest community of living creatures—but none of us quite understood how this could be done. We were too confused to say anything about the possibilities; we could only speak of the things we did not like.

Only two years earlier, Walt probably would have simply thrown out the parts that felt weak. But in those two years he had learned many things, and now he was not misled by our reactions. Where we saw only the faults, he took a positive view of what needed to be done. He asked

In the first presentation of the story sketches, this little skunk drawn by Marc Davis was the most popular character.

imitating the adults. Walt wanted dramatic drawings and exciting scenes which would make the most of the power and grace of these magnificent creatures: a close-up of Bambi's face watching in awe; cut to a long shot as he starts to follow the bucks then turns in panic as they come towards him, leaping over his head and casting shadows on his huddled form. This way the scene made the physical display of grown bucks more personal and accessible to the audience by relating it to the young character they already knew and liked.

We all agreed that these solutions would help, but, "Why does it have to be so real?" the cartoonists asked. Raised on gags and funny sequences, they had trouble finding the entertainment in anything so placidly real.

for even more human touches in the handling of the deer to capture actions the audience would recognize. "I think you can humanize them almost to the point that you humanized Figaro [the kitten in *Pinocchio*]."

The following evening there was a second screening for the full staff of Disney artists. Questionnaires handed out at that showing revealed that the most popular character was the broadly caricatured skunk. "There's the key to the thing," Walt exclaimed.

Bambi's first walk around the neighborhood with his mother received the lowest rating. "Too long, too long!" From the earliest days, Walt had felt this was the way to start his picture, but baby animals with very young voices were failing to excite the audience. He called for more entertaining scenes, stronger characters, and better staging throughout. "Do more caricatures of the animals instead of too straight."

The bucks leaping about on the meadow also received a very low rating. Walt had seen this as an impressive, colorful section and felt that it should be built up instead of being cut. He asked for close-ups of little Bambi trying to show off by

Marc Davis's Bambi and Faline showed that humanized animals gained more sympathy than realistic ones, but cartoonists still asked, "Why does it have to be so real?" (above); Walt defined the medium as putting imagination into the life of the forest (below).

Deer on the meadow as painted by Jules Engel portray the astonishing talent the artists brought to their research.

Actually, it was not a matter of being real instead of entertaining; Bambi would be entertaining because he was real in the audience's mind. It was difficult for us to grasp at the time, but that concept lay at the very heart of the picture we would make. Bambi not only was a deer, he looked like one. He was growing up in a recognizable forest, facing the real problems of survival that confront most wild creatures. Even his childhood friends were believable residents of this neighborhood. Human parallels helped us understand the characters, their personalities, and how they felt about the occurrences in their lives, but for the story to be consistent and moving, the audience had to be convinced that these animals really existed, as animals.

The same was true of Bambi's surroundings. When, years later, the term "magical" was used to describe the forest, John Culhane, author, critic, and animation historian, objected immediately. "The power of it was that is was *real*. It was there. You could walk into it and live with those animals." If there had ever been a question in the audience's mind as to whether the forest and these creatures were true, the hunter's hounds could never have chased Faline, Bambi's mother could not have been shot, and Man could not have been the predator that he was.

Once the audience had been convinced of this reality, there could be richer personality development, broader humor, and more interesting actions. Walt even wondered if the slapstick business they had developed for the bee in Bambi's stomach, and possibly more of the funny squirrel

ABOVE: Faline was often a model for the animators and even patiently endured discussion between Rico Lebrun (standing) *and Eric Larson* (right) *about how she should be drawn. BELOW: Caricatures within the animals held the key to entertainment.*

ABOVE: Faline with her admirers (from left to right) *Louie Schmitt, Ollie Johnston, Milt Kahl, Bill Shull, and Jack Bradbury.*

and chipmunk routines, might not be good additions to the beginning of the picture. "So much . . . cute stuff is swell, but you've got to give them a little punch every once in a while." The punch he wanted would come with the entertaining animation in a few months, but at this time, the story sketches gave the impression that the story could be slow and lacking in entertainment. Many animators wanted no part of this thing, and most could not have done the delicate work that was required. Walt had planned to put more of his key personnel on *Bambi,* but he decided that they would be better cast on the more caricatured personalities in *Alice in Wonderland* and *Peter Pan.* "Those fellows, you know, can do that [type of animation]," he explained. "Milt and Frank and Eric can get down to these fine points. Basically, all the animals throughout *Bambi* are of the cuter type. There's caricature in them, but it's a cuter type of caricature."

Milt had come to the studio from commercial art

work in San Francisco and had animated many scenes of the little animals who helped Snow White through her troubles. Frank had trained for a year with Fred Moore before becoming an animator on his own. Frank's analytical thought and sensitivity had helped him to animate the scenes of the dwarfs crying around Snow White's bier. Eric had animated animals with Milt on *Snow White* and then created the exceptional Figaro in *Pinocchio.* His strength was in his feeling for the natural movements of animals and for their personalities. Eric did not have too much concern for perfection in drawing. He explained, "I knew my animals had to be round and fluffy, and I knew how animals walked and ran because I'd been watching them since I was a kid. But Milt, he'd make the most beautiful drawings you ever saw and pretty soon they'd be down in the wastebasket and he'd be stomping on them. Then he'd be working on another scene and he'd say, 'What did I do with those drawings? Damn! They're down in the waste-

The atmosphere sketches of Ty Wong gave a new direction to the art work and styling of Bambi.

basket!' and he'd pick them out and laugh." A volatile personality went along with his exceptional draftsmanship.

What was so different about us? Why did we think *Bambi* would be such a great project to work on? We knew that Walt was determined to make something very unusual with this story and he was counting on us to bring it to life. Our prime interest was to animate cartoon characters that seemed to be living, to make them believable to an audience, and to involve that audience emotionally with the story. To us, that was the epitome of acting and the greatest challenge to any animator. Could make-believe characters drawn in simple line achieve a theatrical immortality? As we saw it, no artist could be in a better position to do his very best work. Evidently we never questioned our own ability to do it.

In 1939, Walt was demanding an eloquence from

images that he hadn't even imagined before. He was no longer pushing for extra characters, comic situations, and funny attitudes as much as the feelings and sensations we each carry away from visiting the deep woods. He said, "Really, that's our medium—putting imagination into life in the forest." Walt was becoming more certain and more aggressive in his thinking. The experiences on *Pinocchio* and *Fantasia* had helped him grow in his concepts, his vision, and his filmmaking.

When the storymen suggested some minor gags for the early part of *Bambi*'s raindrop sequence, Walt visualized a different approach. "Don't you think it would be better if you held it down . . . not gags—but little pictures?" Everything in the bright sunlight would be happy, the characters would play around, "but now, when it rains—you know, you don't have any birds or anything. What you'd get would be little pictures."

He envisioned simple tableaus of animals in their nests or burrows in the hushed atmosphere of the rain in the forest.

And again, Walt continued his search for eloquence through the use of music.

> This is a picture for music, too. This *Bambi*. It's a natural for it. More than just background music. The whole winter thing—all music. The whole damn hunt—music. Instead of so many sound effects . . . like the fire and everything—do it all with music . . . I think you ought to see what happens to some of that music [in *Fantasia*] when we put action to it.

Walt (left), *Igor Stravinsky* (middle), *and* Bambi *director Bill Roberts* (right) *confer on* Fantasia's *"Rite of Spring," which anticipated the dramatic use of music in* Bambi.

Larry Morey suggested doing the bird calls with flutes and piccolos, but Walt saw larger opportunities. "It's a matter of orchestration. Like Stravinsky—the orchestration—the way he brings all the instruments together and gets his effects from it."

Walt was outlining his current plan for future pictures and how best to use the staff which by now totaled twelve hundred people. On *Bambi* he concluded, "There would be a disaster here if we started rushing everybody in on this picture."

His plans for the three supervising animators, Milt, Frank, and Eric, were that they would know all of the characters and be able to handle any of them throughout the whole picture. They would do the experimental work, finding the right drawing designs and personalities and actions of the animals. When they felt ready, they would bring on the other animators, one at a time as needed. Walt suggested a number of very promising young fellows. "There's a lot of boys coming that look like they're going to really have the stuff." Many talented "boys" were indeed coming along, but Ollie Johnston was the only one who already had the "stuff." Walt had been very impressed with his animation of Pinocchio and had stopped him in the hall once to tell him so. Ollie asserted himself so quickly that he was made the fourth supervising animator on *Bambi* before the experimental work had barely begun.

Ollie had come to the studio from Chouinard's Art School in January of 1935 and been snapped up by the Effects Department seeking men of a careful, conscientious nature. Fortunately, his talents were also recognized by Fred Moore, who needed a replacement in his unit after Frank moved out. Ollie worked with Fred throughout the making of *Snow White*. When that picture was completed, Ollie left Fred to continue on his own as a Disney animator, working up to supervising animator on the cupids and centaurettes in *Fantasia*. Ollie was the most sensitive of the four supervisors on *Bambi* and brought life and captivating personality touches to the animals. He had the ability to somehow get inside their heads and show what they were thinking. He seemed to know instinctively what elements should be in a scene or a sequence to make it communicate clearly with the audience.

While Eric and Ollie were busy finishing up their animation assignments on *Fantasia,* Milt and

OPPOSITE: The supervising animators each brought a special touch to their work: (In rows from top to bottom) *Eric Larson's drawings always had strong attitudes and clear staging; Frank Thomas's stressed acting and personality; Milt Kahl's showed vitality and interesting movement within careful design; and Ollie Johnston's instilled a wonderful sense of emotion.*

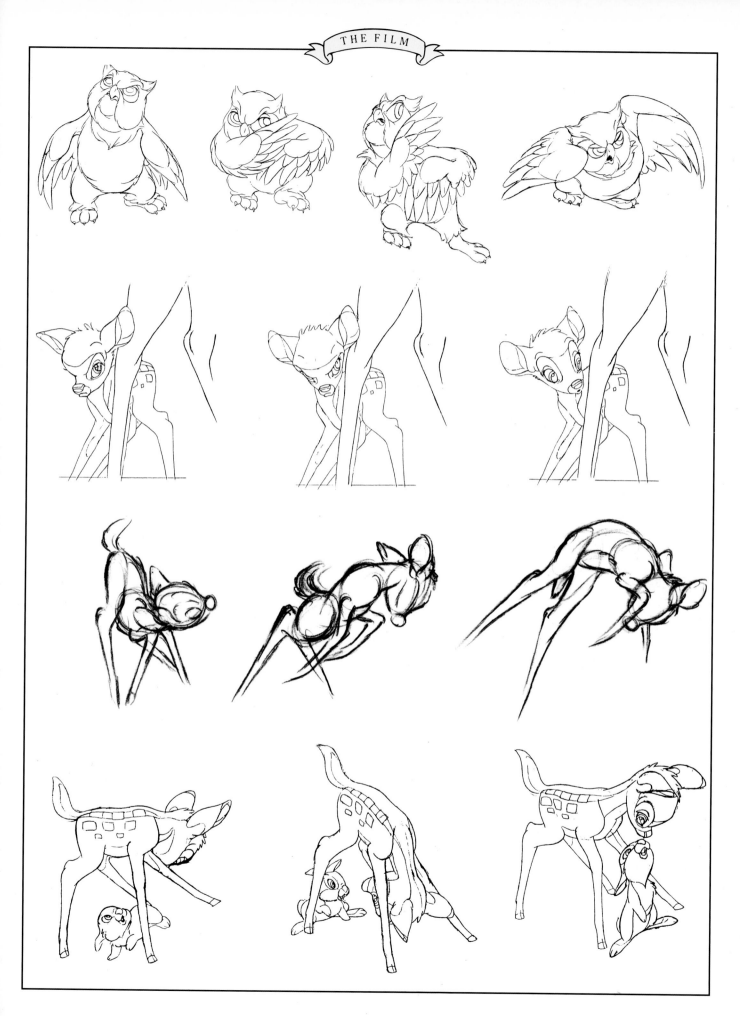

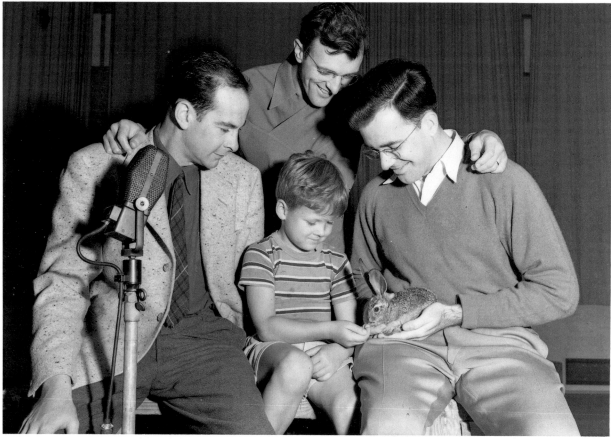

Top: Drawings by (from left to right): Rico Lebrun, Bernard Garbutt, Marc Davis, and Milt Kahl show how the design for Bambi developed from a realistic approach. Above: Ollie

Johnston (left), Milt Kahl (standing), and Frank Thomas (right) introduce Peter Behn, the voice of Thumper, to a real rabbit.

Frank were preparing to start the experimental animation that would prove whether we were now skilled enough to make a feature picture about deer in a forest.

Milt's interest had always been in making realistic, clear, well-organized, beautiful drawings. He thought in terms of interesting patterns of movement more than acting, which usually produced complex body positions and difficult problems of clarity. His was a very personal style that was most difficult for others to duplicate, which subconsciously pleased him. Outwardly, Milt saw his accomplishments only as a combination of a bril-

liant mind and a driving passion to be the best. Marc Davis remembered Milt's attitude: "He never took credit for how good he was—he thought he just worked harder."

Frank was more interested in the inner feelings of the characters, and drawing was merely the means of communicating his ideas. His great strength was in creating a role through acting, striving always to find the gestures, the mannerisms, the expressions, and the interaction between characters which revealed the depth of their engaging personalities. He was dismayed when he had made a good drawing that somehow did not quite fit the acting pattern he wanted. Milt exclaimed, "You can always use a good drawing! Change your pattern."

Frank insisted that the acting came first, then the drawing. Milt snorted, "If the drawing is good, there's no need for acting. The drawing says it all!" Two different philosophies, two different men. But Milt and Frank did agree on what constituted a good drawing and also on the design of each of the characters they were drawing. As Walt had announced, "Kahl and Thomas working together make a good team."

Walt was particularly concerned about how the animators would handle the mouths of the animals in dialogue. How could anyone draw the lip and jaw movement necessary to shape the words without the long, narrow muzzle of an adult deer looking soft and rubbery? In addition, "poetic" lines of

Frank Thomas lent his skill to a caricature of Marian Darlington, who whistled imitations of every bird in the forest for Bambi.

dialogue embarrassed him. Walt wanted a direct, honest approach; he wanted dialogue that reflected the personality of the speaker, and above all, it had to sound natural and entertaining.

We needed to get some animation started as soon as possible. It would not only show just how much of a problem there was with the mouths in dialogue but it would also begin to define each character. Walt said, "We found that out on *Pinocchio*. You don't find your characters until you begin to do a little animation on them."

All the animators had commented on the exceptional voice of the young rabbit, Thumper, but no one in the story crew had expanded his role in the picture. It was only after he had been used in a few places as a solution to larger problems that we began to see his potential for making any scene more lively and entertaining.

The voice belonged to four-year-old Peter Behn, who had first tested for a young animal in November of 1938. He was self-assured without being obnoxious, critical without being sarcastic, bold without being malicious, bossy without being annoying. He also was loud. But his distinctive voice had not been what Perce and his staff were looking for. The director of the recording session said immediately, "Get that kid out of here, he can't act!" But the animators who heard the recording the next day were overjoyed at finding such an unexpected talent and insisted they find Peter Behn and get him back at once.

From the beginning, Bambi's mother had been the one to take her young son around the neighborhood, introducing him to their friends, the quail, the possum, the birds, and the rabbits. This section had always been charming and peaceful—and dull. More than mother's love was needed to make this introduction to our fawn interesting and memorable. It was suggested that perhaps Bambi could be surrounded by bunnies while he watches the birds sing.

FRANK: I like the little bunny teaching him to talk. The bunnies are cute. They're easier to handle than Bambi's mother.

WALT: If you had the little bunny in there when he met the skunk, too.

FRANK: It makes a cute setup to have little Bambi and the bunny and the skunk . . . instead of the great big mother.

WALT: The little bunny can be kind of amused when Bambi calls a butterfly a bird . . . then it keeps getting funnier to him when he calls the skunk a flower—this little bunny laughs like hell.

And now the whole first part of the picture began to be about wonderful children who happened to be animals, innocent and unaware of the realities in their futures. The problems of how to make the adults convincing and interesting disappeared, for they were now supporting players, reacting to the intriguing personalities of the

Bambi's walk through the forest (above and below) *began to be about wonderful children who happened to be animals, innocent and unaware of the realities in their futures.* OPPOSITE: *The memory of young Bambi's experiences would ensure that audiences continued to care about him as he grew older.*

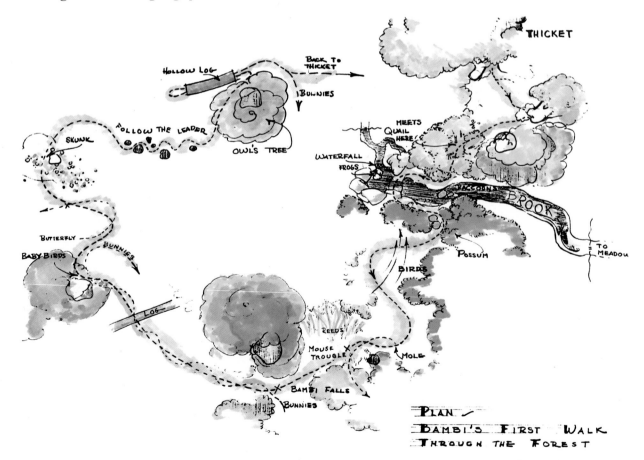

youngsters. The audience would no longer watch the mouths to see if they were really talking, for the focus had shifted to the main characters, and what was being said became more important than how. And the memory of the charming experiences of the young Bambi with his friends, and particularly the sympathy evoked by the death of his mother, would help the audience care for him and the other, less-attractive, grown deer. Suddenly we had something we could animate, entertainment that the whole world understood, the richest and most memorable characters we would ever create.

Thumper became the hit of the show. He was sincere and entertaining, ending the argument that it was impossible to have a straight character be funny, or a comical one be considered real. We only had to be careful to stay within these borders in animating him, so that both the serious and comic moments in the film would fit in.

During a discussion of the big sweep through the forest by the hunters' drive, Perce presented the idea that instead of Mr. Hare being the one who dies, as Sidney Franklin had suggested, "why don't we kill Thumper?" Since Thumper and Bambi had been pals as children, the situation would be much more powerful. From the standpoint of story structure it made sense. Dave Hand was very enthusiastic about the idea and brought it up at each subsequent meeting. Eventually, however, everyone realized that clearly Bambi was the one to be shot and both characters could not share the same problem. Thumper was saved.

By the end of the year, Walt's confidence had already made a great difference in the way *Bambi* looked as a picture. The babbling brook was gone as well as much of the squirrel and chipmunk routines, but there still remained some very sensitive sections that caused the animators nightmares. There were the two leaves asking about the hereafter; the two winds, which were now a part of the romance shared by Faline and Bambi (how do you animate two winds?); and the realistic footage of adult deer running about. On top of that were two of Walt's

favorite sequences: the animals talking about Man, and the charred forest where Bambi learns that Man is not all-powerful. When any of these were mentioned, Milt and Frank exchanged frantic looks and tried to change the subject.

The Old Stag presented a particular problem also. We knew that he was thinking great thoughts of courage and wisdom, but how would anyone in the theater know it? He could not look like he was thinking—we could not put a sparkle in his real deer's eye. We would need some kind of movement, some action that would convince the audience that he was indeed the Great Prince of the forest. The best alternative was to make him the strong, silent man of action. He would sound the alarm when there was danger and lead his herd to safety. Once known and understood by the things he had done, he became stronger and more majestic by saying less. As with the cowboy stars of the 1930s, the deed rather than the speech created the heroic character.

A startling moment for us came when we saw Retta Scott's amazing sketches of the vicious dogs chasing Faline and keeping her cornered on a high ledge. We wondered who at the studio could have drawn this terrifying situation so convincingly and would have guessed that such virile drawings could have been done only by some burly man, probably with a bristling beard and the look of an eagle in his eye. We were amazed to find instead that they were done by a small, delicate, wonderfully cheerful young woman with twinkling eyes and a crown of blonde curls piled on top of her head. Retta was strong, had boundless energy, and drew powerful animals of all kinds from almost any perspective and in any action. No one could match her ability.

When the time came, there was no question but that she would somehow have to do the animation herself. Eric set up the scenes and showed her what needed to be done. With typical modesty, he said, "I worked with her on the timing, but she did it all; she worked and worked on it. This gal had a feeling for movement. . . . She had a feeling for power." Between the two of them there appeared on the screen one of the most chilling and exciting pieces of action ever to be animated.

We knew that the Old Stag was thinking great thoughts, but how would anyone in the theater know it? (top); Bernard Garbutt worked closely with Milt Kahl to create an image of the Great Prince of the Forest as the strong, silent type (above).

Retta Scott's drawings of the vicious dogs who attacked Faline surprised everyone with their potency. She later became the studio's first woman animator.

Many of the backgrounds we were seeing at this time were very detailed, almost to the point of looking like photographs, and we were having a serious problem with the unbroken expanse of flat color on the animated adult deer against such paintings. The sketches of the deer made for the story reels were far more than outlines and even had suggestions of shadows falling across the bodies. They were like book illustrations, with bits of shading to give the illusion of solidity, define the shapes, and help display the expressions. How could it be done in animation? We could not use shading on our drawings—everything had to be done in line backed up by a single color of paint. And how could a background with all the leaves and twigs and details of the forest be balanced against such a large, unrelieved area?

The solution came out of the innovative work of one special artist—Tyrus Wong. His paintings, styling sketches, watercolors, and pastels would give a whole new appearance to the picture, distinct from any we had previously given or would ever give any film.

Ty had come to California from China at the age of nine. When he was hired at Disney, studio policy had every newcomer start as a lowly in-betweener, executing the often-tedious drawings that filled out the action between the animator's key drawings. In Ty's case, it was not a profitable decision. He not only hated the work, but commented that his eyes were beginning to feel like a couple of tennis balls as he flipped the drawings of

Mickey and stared at the light in his drawing board. When he heard that experimental work was being done on *Bambi,* he worked several nights to gather together samples of what he could do. He had read Felix Salten's book and "thought the story was very, very nice—the feeling—you can almost smell the pine." He took his sketches to the art director, Tom Codrick. Like those working for him, Tom had been painting realistically. But when he saw these soft-edged, Oriental paintings of a mystical forest, he realized instantly that this was just what was needed to make *Bambi* a different, artistic picture.

In contrast to the paintings that showed every detail of tiny flowers, broken branches, and fallen logs, Ty had a different approach and certainly one that had never been seen in an animated film before. He explained, "Too much detail! I tried to keep the thing very, very simple and create the atmosphere, the feeling of the forest." His grasses were a shadowy refuge with just a few streaks of the actual blades; his thickets were soft suggestions of deep woods and patches of light that brought out the rich detail in the trunk of a tree or a log. Groups of delicate trees were shown in

silhouette against the mists of early morning rising from the meadow. Every time of day and each mood of the forest was portrayed in a breathtaking manner. An ethereal quality was there. Best of all, Walt was enthusiastic. "I like that indefinite effect in the background—it's effective. I like it better than a bunch of junk behind them."

Marc Davis said, "The influence Ty had on this film *made* the film! . . . Taking these complicated things with eight million leaves . . . he was able to find a way of putting these things together so you felt the dampness and the moisture of everything in the forest, but you didn't draw every single leaf—they were beautiful."

When asked about his style, Ty said, "Halfway between the West and the East—but I can't help that, I'm born with it." He set the color schemes along with the appearance of the forest in painting after painting, hundreds of them, depicting Bambi's world in an unforgettable way. Here at last was the beauty of Salten's writing, created not in a script or with character development, but in paintings that captured the poetic feeling that had eluded us for so long.

In spite of the questionable sections that were still part of the picture, Milt and Frank were eager to get started. At the end of December they became the first two artists at Disney's new animation building in Burbank, arriving at the same time as the air-conditioning units. One day they were sweltering in temperatures around 115°F and the next near freezing while the equipment was being tested and the thermostats installed. Their first drawings of Bambi showed the young star either as a roast piglet with an apple in his mouth or as a frozen image in a cake of ice.

Milt and Frank attacked the mountain of research material that had been accumulated, carefully studying the photographs, the sketches, and the comparative anatomy. Any actor would have won praise for a performance based on such well-conceived material as that developed by our story crew. The advance work was paying off, leaving the animators free to concentrate on timing, movements, acting, and a feeling of life.

Ty Wong, whose artistic style influenced the entire look of the film. OPPOSITE: In contrast to such paintings as Gustaf Tenggren's (top) that showed every detail, Ty Wong had a different approach (bottom). PAGES 154 TO 157: Ty Wong's atmosphere sketches gave a new direction to the art and styling of Bambi, using a broad range of color and a variety of locales, but always with a delicate, slightly mysterious feeling. To capture and re-create the delicate shading of Ty's originals, many of the background painters had to switch from gouache to oil paints. Charles Solomon, critical reviewer of animation for the Los Angeles Times, *said of Ty Wong's paintings, "He shows you less of what you would see and more of what you feel looking at a forest."*

Pure Gold

Those personalities are just pure gold.
— WALT DISNEY

The Nazi blitzkrieg of 1939 had quickly destroyed our very lucrative foreign market, but if Walt was worried about money, he did not show it. At the studio, excitement was high, for *Pinocchio* would soon be running in the theaters, *Bambi* would be in animation, and all the employees would be together once more at the wonderful new studio.

In 1936, when the first meetings were held on *Bambi,* the animals we were drawing for our short films looked more like designs for toy manufacturers than convincing creatures of the forest, and the animation itself was stiff and very simple. In 1940 our animation was much smoother, expressive, rich in storytelling and communication; it added great visual drama to every segment of the films. In *Fantasia,* the glorious music of the *Rite of Spring* and *Night on Bald Mountain* showed the kind of emotional strength we could expect in our *Bambi* sequences. With the anticipated revenues from our lavish second feature, *Pinocchio,* we would be able to make *Bambi* truly exquisite.

Everybody stopped work on the seventh of February, the day that *Pinocchio* was released across the United States. It was a disaster! In spite of glowing memories of *Snow White and the Seven Dwarfs,* just over two years earlier, people were more concerned with the approaching war

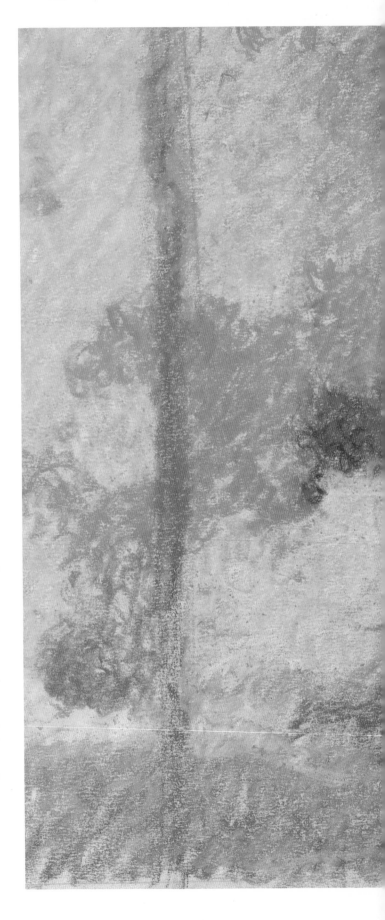

The visual drama of the research paintings such as this magnificent forest by Harold Miles was now being translated into animation and technical effects.

than with the adventures of a wooden boy. The most beautiful and expensive cartoon ever made up to that time failed to bring in a profit at the box office. It was a terrible blow.

Most of the studio's animators were now working on *Fantasia.* Milt and Frank were well into their experimental animation on the young fawn, having studied miles of film and talked to the sketch men who had been drawing deer for more than a year. Dave Hand recalled, "*Bambi* was a most difficult picture to animate because of [the] anatomical construction of the deer. All the key animators were taking special instruction in deer actions, all of it most difficult. I felt sorry for them and the problem they had to meet."

There was film of our live Bambi and Faline, taken while they were young and frisky, which was very helpful. Still, they had no expressions, no smiles, no eyebrows or fat cheeks. They would have to be humanized a great deal to achieve the success of Eric's kitten in *Pinocchio*.

A smaller muzzle and much larger cranium finally created the new design that made all of the expressions available to the animators. The men trained under Bernard Garbutt were startled and dismayed. After spending a year perfecting a realistic design, it seemed to them that these anima-

tors still had much to learn, for at the very least, they had certainly failed to notice the shape and construction of any young deer. Behind the animators' backs Garby's men smiled at Bambi, the "little pumpkin-head."

Eventually, Frank and Milt had each animated approximately one hundred feet of the young Bambi and Thumper. The footage ran just over two minutes, but they were satisfied enough to show it to Walt. The meeting was on March 1, 1940, possibly the most important day in the whole history of the film.

Four years of doubt, of questioning whether this could be done, was now on the line. The realistic yet humanized deer that Marc Davis had designed; the mysterious paintings of Ty Wong that would bring the audience into the picture through their own imaginations; the amazing voice of Peter Behn, so full of character and so unusual

in sound; all hung on the ability of two men to breathe life—even more than life—into drawings. Animated characters must be created to communicate story ideas in the most entertaining way. Just being alive was not enough.

Walt seldom gave a direct compliment, letting us feel that sheer perfection was the standard he expected, but at this meeting he made an exception. After seeing the footage, he turned to the two animators with tears in his eyes and said, "Thanks, fellows, that's great stuff, no kidding. Those personalities are just pure gold." What had been attractive drawings for so long were now living characters with personalities and feelings.

He particularly liked the gentle flow of the action in contrast to the frenetic feeling of so many animated scenes. "I like that easy pace where you are not hurrying—where you take time. You have value there . . . you don't have to go at that terrific pace to cover up." We treasured most these words: "It's your picture. You guys have a feeling for this picture. You belong to this picture."

Walt was particularly pleased with the pacing of the action, which flowed rather than raced at the frenetic speed of earlier films (above); *As well as merely seeming alive, animated characters now had to communicate story ideas in the most entertaining way* (below). OPPOSITE: *In 1940, the animated Thumper* (left) *was richer in storytelling and character than the work done for* Little Hiawatha *in 1937* (right), *and more sophisticated than the early bunny sketches for* Bambi (middle).

He stressed again the importance of working with a small crew, just the right people who "are not going to be weights around your neck." In April, Eric and Ollie were moved from their assignments on *Fantasia* to start animating sequences on *Bambi*. They were soon joined by Garby and Marc Davis, the two outstanding story sketch men who seemed to have the best feeling for drawing animals. It was a harsh introduction to animation for these two talented artists.

Walt had always liked Garby's naturalistic drawings and wondered if he could with some help animate the more realistic scenes in the picture: long shots of deer walking, the bucks leaping about on the meadow, the animals running in panic during the drive and the fire. Garby had probably expected more, but we had gone so far from his original suggestions that he had trouble enough with the motions and characters so different from the ones he had designed. Eric helped him with the timing and the arrangement of his drawings and found a good assistant to adapt his drawings to the current model.

Marc also was thrust into animation unexpectedly. One day while Walt was looking at some story sketches done by Marc, he had said, "I like these sketches. I want to see those drawings on the screen. Have Milt Kahl and Frank Thomas teach him how to animate." Marc recalled, "That's how I became an animator." In time he became a top animator, but whenever he had trouble with a scene he would say, "This is your fault! Walt told you guys to teach me to animate and you didn't do it."

Years later, film critic Peter Stack of the *San Francisco Chronicle* asked, "How did a bunch of young cartoon artists in a town called Hollywood ever capture, in such perfect lines and detail, the rhythms and gracefulness of deer?" And Marc was once asked how we managed to animate this film without the help of rotoscope (to trace images from frames of live action film). His response answers both questions: "We just had a small group . . . who could handle it."

It was most fortunate that our picture was structured with the young animals at the start of the story and that we had chosen to do our experi-

It was fortunate that the film and also the experimental animation began with the young animals, providing the opportunity to develop the characters in the most appealing ways. Establishing similar attraction for the adult animals without that foundation would have proved an impossible task (top, above, and opposite).

162

mental animation on that section, because it had given us the opportunity to develop our characters in situations that were the most appealing to the audience. If the story had begun with the grown deer, we would have had an almost impossible task establishing a similar attraction for the viewers.

By late spring the whole mood at the studio had changed. The depression over *Pinocchio* had lifted somewhat, and now *Bambi* was accepted as not only a true work of art but a very entertaining picture. There were still many problems to be solved, but that was normal for a feature film. The important thing was that everyone was excited about the prospects. We were creating the biggest, warmest, most beautiful, most impressive show that would ever be seen. *Fantasia* was longer but it did not have the story or the acting and personalities that we had here. At well over nine thousand feet in length, *Bambi* would transport the audience to an emotionally charged forest for an hour and forty-five minutes of artistry, humor, and incredible action.

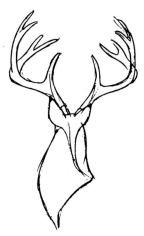

The most difficult animation problem was how to successively draw the stag's antlers as his head turned, without their appearing to continuously writhe and twist. Bob Jones invented the system of photographing a three-dimensional model and tracing the antlers onto animation drawings, thereby creating fixed, regal antlers for the Great Prince of the Forest, animated by Don Lusk (above) and Bernard Garbutt (below).

Each of the studio's departments had developed a fierce pride and professional approach to their work after the challenges they had met on the last two pictures; they could do anything, given a bit of time and a priority. Every time we thought we had been completely stopped, someone would come up with a solution, usually something never done before and, as it turned out, never done again. It seemed that nothing could stop *Bambi* now. ⁓

The most difficult problem to resolve was the one known as the "rubber antlers." When discussing ways to make the Old Stag look impressive and commanding, no one had ever thought of how the rigid, complex set of horns could be animated. No one had ever considered that it might be difficult to do. The Great Prince of the forest had to be the most magnificent and heroic figure anyone could draw, and that required as awesome an array of antlers as ever crowned a stag in any forest.

Yet no one could project both in mind and on paper the perspective changes of the bony structure as the majestic head turned. While each indi-

vidual drawing looked correct, in movement the antlers slithered into a rubbery substance that refused to remain either stiff or regal. This could have meant the end of the picture just as everything was beginning to fall into line. How could we present our great, stately stag without antlers? For a creature who needed such an imposing appearance, such mystical feeling, it would have been completely unacceptable.

It was Bob Jones, our fledgling engineer, who figured out the ingenious solution. Build a model of the antlers, reflect the image through a mirror onto the drawings of the deer's head, film it, then trace the resulting combination onto our drawings. Success! The model could be turned in any direction to match the movement of the animation, and while the process was a bit tedious, it was not nearly as demanding—or unpromising—as the attempt to draw the antlers just from imagination. Bob had preserved the believability needed for the stag to play out his dramatic role.

The Effects Department had expanded to over one hundred and twenty artists and their work had become an integral part of every film, contributing drama and excitement and mood, as well as believability. New technical advances and Walt's inspiring interest opened the way for these animators to add their own artistry to that of nature. Walt described a forest fire he had seen, "I don't mean to humanize the things—but you watch a fire . . . you can still keep it as flames and everything, but by God, they're hungry. They're reaching for things. It's when they blow from one branch to another—I don't mean to put hands on them, but there's a force to a fire. There's something alive to a fire . . . it has a feeling of a very hungry beast that's out there devouring everything in its way." Any animator would know what to do after hearing such a description.

Between Walt's support and the technical assistance available, all of the special needs of *Bambi* could be handled: falling raindrops shown from any angle, clouds, sunsets, dripping water, mist, flames, shotgun blasts, and even wind sweeping across a grassy field. In a lovely scene of a meadow bathed in moonlight, a gentle breeze bends each blade of grass low as it passes over, creating

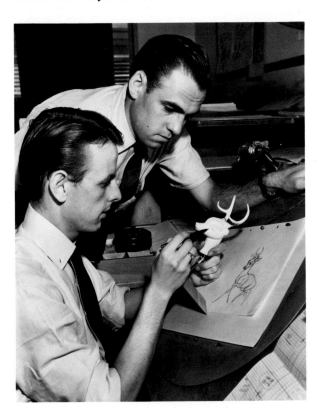

Willie Pyle (left) *and Lee Morehouse* (right) *study the model which solved the problem of the "rubber antlers."*

a pattern of changing light that follows the course of the moving air. The question of how to animate the two winds had been answered.

Walt kept pushing his musicians and criticizing their work as well. He pointed out, "The music has to give dramatic emphasis and I feel a monotony through it. . . . The way this picture is designed, you haven't told it with dialogue—you've got to do it with music. . . . I tell you it will add to the picture's greatness if you do have a marvelous musical score, one that really expresses the action and gives force to it. . . . [*Fantasia*] has proven this much. Even if the thing is a flop, we'll have gained a thorough appreciation of what can be done with music."

This skillful integration of music and visuals was one of the most important ingredients in making *Bambi* work so well. The excitement of the bucks leaping on the meadow, the threat of Man approaching, the April shower, the innocence of the very young Bambi, the terrible drive by the hunters and the fire that followed—each of these were animated, matching the feeling of the music to the actions of the characters. This could not have been done after *Snow White,* with its memorable songs, or even after *Pinocchio,* but the work on *Fantasia* had developed the musical skills we were now using. This type of musical treatment helped create the moods found in the original *Bambi* book and transposed to the film the special emotions felt by the reader.

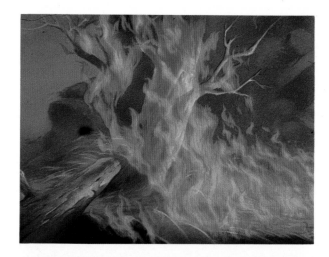

Time and again Walt had tried to re-create the haunting moments of the two last leaves on a tree discussing the end of their lives. Most of us felt that this memorable part of Salten's book was not right for animation, but Walt had wanted to build that section of his film into a dramatic transition of fall turning into winter. After three years of trying, he finally decided against it.

"I can't conceive of the leaves being as effective in the picture as it was in the book," Walt said. He knew that animation was a medium of imagery and graphics and by now believed that strong artwork

Walt's description of a forest fire as a living thing, devouring everything in its way, stimulated the animators to create more expressive actions and scenery. OPPOSITE: *The remarkable paintings of Ty Wong not only inspired the other visual artists, but created a standard that was met by musicians and special effects too.*

Walt tried desperately to keep the dialogue of the last two leaves of autumn in the film, but finally let the poignant images speak for themselves.

supported by music would do far more than hushed dialogue. Thus, the animated images of the last two leaves on a barren tree, trembling in the cold wind, then finally losing their hold on the branch that had nourished them, depicted the end of their lives in a very touching way. They swirled in the wind briefly then settled on the earth where they lay peacefully together. No one in the theater missed the meaning when it was told in such a tender, graphic form.

After such a moment, the picture needed to lift its spirits once more, and Walt concentrated on making something out of the snowfall. Instead of a few cold flakes adding to the melancholy beauty of this scene, the snow should be saved for the next

morning, so Bambi could get the surprise that Walt remembered as a boy. "A kid . . . goes to sleep at night and then he wakes up in the morning and looks out and the ground is blanketed with snow. I'll never forget the thrill I got out of it." The rest of that meeting was all about how kids play in the snow and fall into deep drifts and try to dodge the clumps of snow that fall off the trees. These were all things an audience would understand. It would awaken happy memories.

Another favorite part of Salten's book was the argument between the forest animals and a dog about Man and his power. The dog explains why he killed the fox and why it was so wonderful to do Man's bidding. In our version, the single dog had

become four or five, and Walt said, "I would take time on those dogs. I think that's a swell section . . . because it's a question you ask all the time. Here Man has animals and goes out and hunts animals. . . . There's a reason: the dog believes in Man. These animals can't understand why."

Gradually this idea had developed into the sequence of the pack of vicious hounds keeping Faline trapped on a ledge by leaping and snapping at her. Walt talked about the way he saw it. "They've got her now, you know. Man will be there pretty soon. That's what they do. 'We go out and track 'em.' You could even build that with the little squirrels . . . the squirrels see them [men] coming and say, LET HER GO. YOU HAVE GOT TO LET HER GO. HERE HE COMES. They plead with the dogs to let her go, and dogs won't. . . . You begin to root for these little characters in the forest. They're sticking up for Faline. They're in danger of their own lives, but they stay and try to get Faline released."

But the words of the squirrels were having no effect on the dogs and could scarcely be heard above the growling and barking, which was so much more gripping. The play between the tame and the wild creatures had been lost in the drama of the situation, and Walt's attempts to keep some small portion of the feeling only got in the way. When it was determined that this was the one place where Bambi could be a hero, the emphasis of the sequence was changed. The dogs attacked without interruption from Faline's friends. There was still suspense from the possibility that Man would arrive any minute, but the frightening visuals of Bambi attacking the threatening dogs all by himself created a much stronger element of tension. Emotionally, it was a high point, seared in our memories.

Walt wanted impact and a feeling of realism, but he didn't like to see ugliness and cruelty or dying animals. During the panic of the hunters' drive, the animals who were shot were hit offstage, out of view of the audience. There were only near misses when we actually saw the fleeing animals and birds on the screen, darting about, stopping as gun blasts ripped holes in logs and dirt, then scurrying on again. Bambi was the sole character to be hit by a bullet before the audience's eyes.

Another dialogue that was finally dropped from the film had the forest animals trying to talk Man's dogs into letting Faline go. Instead, Bambi's valor strengthened the visual drama.

There were constantly recurring discussions about the sequence where Bambi's mother was shot. It seemed like a fairly obvious proposition with little to question, but many nuances had to be considered.

Milt wanted a long buildup with a blizzard becoming more intense so that the shot would come during the greatest hardship, as Bambi and his mother are huddled together. Walt felt that was wrong. "You don't want a blizzard when she gets shot. Wouldn't it be better to build the feeling up and then finally have relief, and just as there's relief, then comes this other thing?"

We all agreed that more should be made of the lack of food during the winter so that the discovery of the new spring grass would have greater importance. Perce had suggested that Bambi should find the grass and start to eat, then think of his mother and rush back to tell her. Walt said, "Don't you think Bambi's mother ought to find that grass? It shows her feeding her young, taking care of him. . . . It's just before she gets killed, and it makes you feel he's more helpless and everything." He added, "They've found grass. It means that winter is nearly over. In other words, they've gone through the danger."

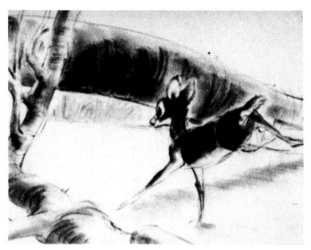

After detecting Man's presence, they run for the protection of the thicket; the mother would hold back to shield Bambi, while urging him to run faster. This seemed too clumsy to portray so we settled on the two of them running as fast as they could, with the mother calling, "Don't look back!" They come to a log lying over the path and Bambi darts underneath. The mother leaps over the log, going out the top of the frame, and at that moment the shot is heard and her crumpled form falls into the scene on the far side of the log. She lies motionless.

Bambi arrives at the thicket feeling they are safe, but his mother is not around. He starts back, but by the time he has reached the log, the body is gone with only the imprint in the snow where she had fallen. Possibly there are still the marks where she has been dragged away. This worried Walt.

LEFT TO RIGHT: The continuity as developed on the storyboard shows Bambi eating the new spring grass, giving the feeling that the hardship of winter is over, then running in terror with his mother as they sense that Man is near. Bambi ducks under a

*log and runs off, but his mother leaps over it and out of the
frame. A shot is heard and her body falls into the scene.
Eventually Walt realized that this would be too much for the
audience and those drawings were taken out.*

WALT: He doesn't know where she is and starts coming back, but you don't come back to her, do you?

LARRY: We come back to the image in the snow.

WALT: Do you have to do that?

PERCE: It's powerful.

WALT: I was just wondering if we even had to do that?

LARRY: It sounded pretty good, Walt.

WALT: No blood.

LARRY: No, just the imprint.

WALT: You know she's dead, but the little guy just comes back to that thing and the snow begins to pick up and he's crying, MOTHER! and it would just tear their hearts out if we could get that little guy crying MOTHER, but this blizzard comes—this little fellow in the blizzard—and right out of the blizzard comes this stag, you know. You never come back and show the imprint of the mother. It's all by suggestion.

They all thought this over and Walt asked, "Do you think it's too sad, too gripping? It's powerful . . . I just wonder if coming back and seeing her form isn't just sticking a knife in their hearts." He tried talking it through another way to see how it would sound. "He starts following those tracks, which [are] . . . the Man's tracks, and where the deer has been dragged—getting frantic, falling into snow, getting deep into snow, and building up, and the wind begins to blow there, and pretty soon someone speaks to him, and he stops. He looks up and there's that stag up there."

Walt did not like that continuity either. "He's hunting for his mother, and he never finds her. . . . It stops any awkward business of him seeing his mother's form and starting any extra crying." But he liked the idea of Bambi stopping with a "sort of scared take. Because you think it might be Man . . . and we cut, and through that haze of snow we see the shadow which is the form of the

Walt decided it would be better to build dramatic tension with Bambi's mother discovering new spring grass (top) *after the long winter's diet of bark* (opposite); *"Just as there's relief, then comes this other thing."* (above).

Winter in the forest set the scene for the harshest lesson of Bambi's young life.

Stag and then we hear him speak, YOUR MOTHER CAN'T BE WITH YOU ANY MORE."

Perce continued the planned dialogue. "MAN HAS TAKEN HER AWAY. I KNOW IT'S HARD TO UNDERSTAND, BUT THAT'S THE WAY OF LIFE IN THE FOREST. NOW YOU'LL HAVE TO BE BRAVE AND WALK ALONE."

Walt asked, "Why couldn't he say, YOU'VE GOT TO LEARN TO WALK ALONE. . . . The Stag takes him and teaches him to walk alone. . . . He believes you have to take things as they come and face facts. That's his philosophy—the philosophy of anyone who is going to survive in the forest."

As they discussed the importance of each line, they were all afraid the scene would be embarrassing with such long speeches. Gradually they cut out one line after the other. First to go was the one that started, "I know it's hard to understand." Then the first two lines about Bambi's mother and Man taking her away were cut to a simple, "Your mother is gone." Last to go were the lines about being brave and walking alone.

But finally, the first line of dialogue was reinstated, though with a warning from Walt to be sure

The softly falling snow created a powerful effect as Bambi meets the Great Prince of the Forest, and leaves his childhood behind.

that the Stag "doesn't have to move much." He would just loom up out of this hazy blizzard and say in a soft, kindly voice, "Your mother can't be with you any more." Walt continued, "And as the Stag goes off, why this little guy is going along there, trying to be brave and going on off into this blizzard, following this big stag. . . . And pretty soon, they have disappeared and there is nothing but this snow falling."

Fantasia was released November 13, but only to the few theaters equipped with Fantasound, Disney Studio's sound system developed for the film. The expense of leasing and converting theaters in selected areas was more than the film's revenues in too many cases. From the first night its future was unsure. Instead of instant success, acclaim, and revenue, we had foreboding signs of another animation classic failing to pay for itself.

Man in the Forest

I'm getting so I don't know. I can't trust my own judgment. I like the stuff.

—WALT DISNEY

In spite of the enthusiasm at the studio, serious problems were developing for *Bambi,* for the studio, and for the world. Walt had always tried to shelter his personnel from the daily problems of running the studio in order to prevent nagging worries from competing with creative energies. Consequently, we had moved into the new studio, designed for the greatest possible creative output, unaware that Walt's days of prosperity had started to wane.

On *Bambi,* only one sequence remained to be developed and moved into animation. That was the charred forest, the all-important sequence in which Bambi realizes that there is a power over all, even over Man. In Felix Salten's book, there were no charred remains and no fire, but the philosophic concept was critical. Walt had always considered this to be the big finish of his film, the point we had been working toward in all of Bambi's training.

Part of the problem facing us was the idea of showing the dead hunter lying in the ashes, killed by his own carelessness. Such a vision of death had never been attempted in an animated film before, and no audience was prepared for it. Pinocchio had been killed while saving his father from the enraged whale, but that had been all fantasy from the beginning. This was real.

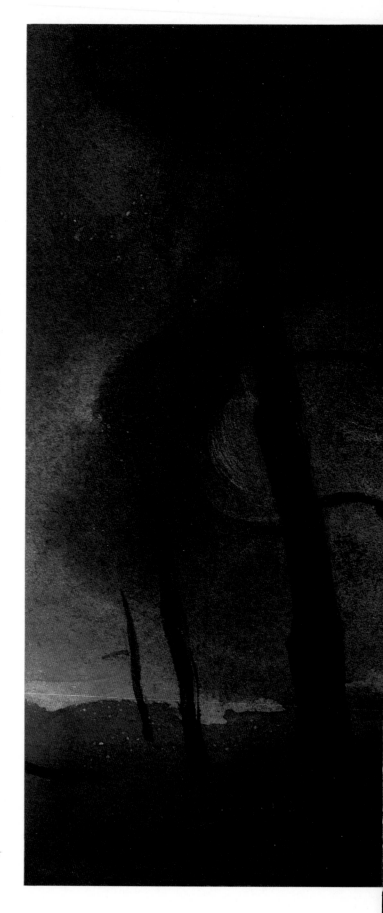

Most imagined the charred forest scene with the remains of the fire cold and lifeless, but in Maurice Noble's painting, the sky is still black with smoke and dying embers still glow in the distance.

WALT: I think you can show a form. You can show a burnt tree. You can show a hand. You can show a hat—a gun—.

DAVE HAND: I think we ought to show the body of Man there. That gun doesn't do it for me.

WALT: I was wondering if it could be almost a silhouette effect of a form. You wouldn't see any details to speak of . . . you feel the human form.

Walt left that thought to consider the deer. "Out of the fog looms these two forms of these two deer, and you come right upon them, and they're standing there, looking down at something . . . the stag says, THERE HE IS. Bambi says, HE'S DEAD. . . . They don't have to fear him now."

Perce read the dialogue again. "The stag says, NO, MAN IS NOT THE FORCE BEHIND ALL THINGS, and he turns to Bambi, DO YOU UNDERSTAND? Bambi answers, I THINK I DO—THERE IS ANOTHER WHO IS OVER US ALL, OVER US—AND OVER HIM. And you hear this faint starting of just barely audible rain—musically. And the stag stands for a moment, NOW YOU ARE READY. THE TIME HAS COME FOR YOU TO TAKE MY PLACE IN THE FOREST, and the rain is coming down very softly. GOODBYE, MY SON."

It was a touching scene, but still had problems. Walt said, "I'd make them pure silhouette forms. Lay off of any details. . . . It's a swell way to handle the mood of this thing. It demands this, and also you're in an awkward thing where these deer might look terrible if you tried to get them dramatic." Adult deer still had not proven as successful as hoped, even when animated by the top men. They were excellent in distant shots, with power and grace, but the acting and crucial expression did not communicate positively.

The meeting broke up with no resolution on how to show Man or how to show the deer during their long passages of dialogue. A screening before a new audience might help us make these important decisions, so a night showing for people from outside the studio was arranged. Walt was reluctant to select one drawing from the dozens that had been made indicating just how Man should be shown. Dave chose the clearest and most specific one and had it placed in the reel, claiming that we would find out what to do, even if it were only to eliminate that particular drawing.

The audience had been enjoying the show, but as the charred forest sequence came on the screen they seemed to be nervous and unsure. It appeared to be too slow and ponderous after the excitement of the fire. Suddenly, Dave's picture of the dead hunter appeared on the screen and four hundred people shot straight up into the air.

Walt's reaction was not just critical of Dave, he wanted the whole sequence cut out of the picture.

The artists were now familiar with capturing the drama of the animals' lives, in such detail as David Hall's (top) and also more simply (above), but still faced a dilemma about the artistic representation of Man. OPPOSITE: Many sketches had been made of the hunter killed in his own fire, but they were either too gruesome or too vague.

Ty Wong created a memorable portrait of a majestic and mysterious Bambi, who lived to become Prince of the Forest.

That left us with no ending for the film, or so it seemed. Didn't Bambi have to learn one last thing? Wasn't he supposed to replace the stag as the Great Prince of the forest? In one story meeting after another we tried to find a grand summation of our whole film. But, it wasn't necessary. Simplicity was the most effective. Rather than have such a moody section right after the devastating fire, we should go for the contrast of the bright, new growth in the forest the following spring and the introduction of Bambi's children with their mother in the thicket.

From the gathering of the friendly animals congratulating Faline on her twins, the camera swings up to show Bambi and the stag, majestically posed, looking down at the tender scene below.

The two deer exchange looks for a moment, then the stag turns and walks away, leaving Bambi alone on top of the hill. Dave exclaimed with relief in his voice, "That does it for me!"

Back at the beginning of the project, Sidney Franklin had told us, "The audience loves to feel they have seen a cycle completed." Eric had also felt that the life cycle idea was very important and left the audience with the feeling that life goes on and still has its beautiful, rewarding moments.

Felix Salten's *Bambi* had featured a central character but the story's theme was more important: how a fawn gained enough wisdom from his experiences in the forest to take the place of the Old Prince. Since Man was the chief threat to the deer throughout their lives, it was essential that

Bambi learn there was someone even greater than Man. Salten needed this expression of his belief in order to reach a summation of his idea for the book. Our version was the story of a particular deer from birth to maturity and the birth of his own children. It did not stress what he learned from the incidents in his life as much as it let the audience see what life was like for this one deer.

The detailed beauty of the forest as portrayed in David Hall's drawing (top) *was distilled into animation* (above).

I n the weeks that followed, we began to understand that at least part of Walt's desire to simplify the charred forest and eventually cut it out completely had been motivated by economics. The studio's financial problems were growing worse. The money from *Snow White* had all been spent, the extremely expensive *Pinocchio* left us with unpaid loans, our new building was not paid for, and *Fantasia* continued to do poorly. Walt had been cutting back bit by bit for a full year, yet there was still more money going out than coming in. A drastic move had to be made. Walt was a fighter and usually full of creative ideas, but now he was trapped; even he could see that there was no way to continue making *Bambi* the way he had planned. What could he do—shelve it and wait for better times before finishing it? Would he still have a studio capable of such a production? Would he have anything left if he cut the budget drastically?

One sad day he called his key animators and directors together and explained the situation. We had to cut expenses, not just a little here and there, but in half. He tried to insist that enough good animation already had been done to carry the picture, and finally admitted that there would be no picture at all if we didn't do something extreme.

We looked at each other bleakly. Frank had tears in his eyes and Walt leaned over to him with unexpected gentleness. "Frank, I know it hurts you, but dammit, it's got to go, that's all there is to it." We had never thought of our work as a mere job. It was far too personal. The thought of losing

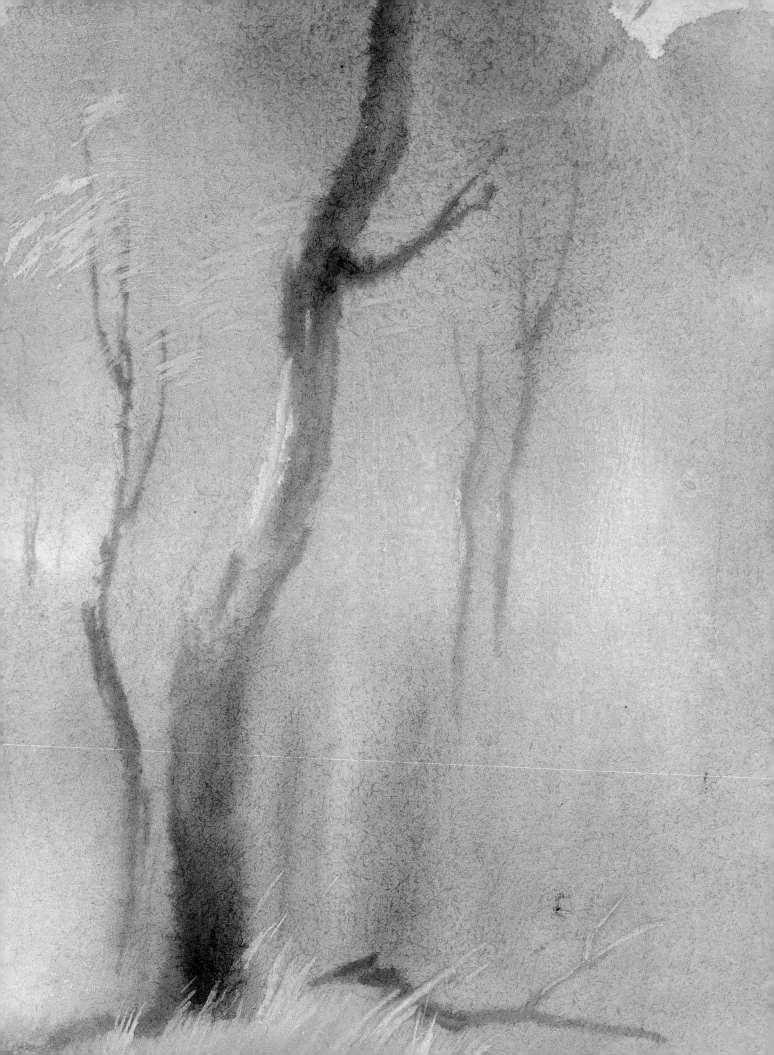

any part of it or of changing the picture into a lesser product was too painful to face. But if we were to save anything we would have to start at once looking for places to trim.

We tried to work faster, put in overtime, get the scenes done by using every shortcut we knew. Taking out the charred forest removed 300 feet from the work yet to be done, and other cuts here and there had taken out 200 more, but the picture still totaled about 8,500 feet with many scenes left to be animated. We limped along this way trying to find acceptable alternatives, but within a few weeks Walt had worked out his own plan to complete the picture.

Don't trim—eliminate! Don't fuss with details—cut out the whole scene. "Cut where there are a million animals." Cut, cut, cut. We were down to 8,000 feet.

There should be no compromising on key scenes of personality or acting or storytelling, but check any section that involves characters in expensive actions. Instead of eight scenes of Bambi and the stag running from the fire, use five. Cut, cut, cut. 7,500 feet.

Cut the additional scenes of effects animation, we have enough now. Cut the scenes that will require careful work and special handling, we don't need more. Cut the moving shadows and changing colors, they slow the pacing of the film. Cut the subtle nuances. Be bold. 6,500 feet.

Possibly the picture worked better without the additional opulence that had been planned. Now it was simpler, more direct, and faster moving. Maybe we were chipping away the husk, the outer layers, the excesses, until we found the core, the pure heart of the subject. Instead of an awesome, majestic, overwhelming experience in the theater, we would offer a jewel. Walt's directives cut more than footage from the film; they cut tedium. They

As almost a third of the picture fell to the cutting room floor, the mystery and subtlety of the poetic depictions of the forest were in danger of being forgotten.

added spirit and texture to a lumbering giant. Walt had a vision that would save this complex artistic venture, but we were still uncertain.

The last of the cuts brought the overall footage on the picture down to 6,259 feet, most of which was already animated. Would there be enough money now to finish what was left? *The Reluctant Dragon* had been completed for only six hundred thousand dollars and released in June, but it did not recover its cost. Now everything depended on *Dumbo,* which was due for release late in the year. Walt told Frank Capra, "If this picture doesn't go over, I'm through!" He meant it.

At that time, we lived from one feature film to the next, with no Disneyland or TV shows or elaborate merchandising to bring in extra revenue. Walt wanted desperately to keep this special crew of talented artists together, but it was simply no longer possible. He knew that if he let them go now, he would never get them back. There were many unpleasant and unfortunate decisions to be made. Could the staff now totaling thirteen hundred be cut in half? Who should be laid off? Who would be next? And what would the future hold for those who stayed? Morale was sinking at the very time we needed the strongest resolve and dedication.

Walt had always had a very personal relationship with the members of his staff. This worked when there were fewer than four hundred employees, but once we had more than one thousand, communications broke down. There were too many who did not know him, had never been in a meeting with him. Though Walt's paternal attitude had provided us with the finest working conditions of any group of artists, quick growth had brought inequities in salaries and questions of how money was being spent. On *Bambi* there were many questions that the supervising animators simply could not answer.

A screen cartoonists' union had just been ratified at the MGM animation studio and was currently organizing at Warner Bros. A small group began to talk of its advantages at Disney Studio. One day the union organizers came to Walt's office, pounded on his desk, and threatened to turn the studio into a dust bowl unless he signed with them. Walt answered that it was up to his employees, that he had no right to sign them over to any union and they would have to have a vote. The response was interesting. "We might lose that way. If we strike, we know we will win." The strike was called on May 29, 1941.

The emotional stress on both sides was enormous. A great schism had developed between those who had cause for criticism of the studio and those who simply believed in Walt. One striker admitted, "I never expected anyone who knew Walt personally . . . to come out on strike." For those who stayed inside, shock and bitterness made creative work extremely difficult.

Walt was stunned. It was almost impossible for him to understand the multilayered reasoning behind a disturbing comment or action because he had always taken things personally. He was assured that it would all be over in a matter of days, but his advisors were wrong. One day he sadl· commented, "The spirit that played such an important part in the building of the cartoon medium has been destroyed."

With each passing week, there were insults and distortions of fact thrown about carelessly, and Walt, frustrated and infuriated, and the victim of unfounded personal attacks, could see no way of salvaging any of his dreams from the past. Production gradually came to a complete stop.

The studio closed in mid-August while the government arbitrator worked out the settlement. When the studio reopened on September 12, it was unionized. For every three employees who had stayed in, two strikers were brought back. Thus, a large portion of strikers returned, while close to a hundred of those who had stayed were without jobs. It was an unsettling arrangement which left everybody dissatisfied.

However, Walt was determined to move ahead. When he was asked, "How are we ever going to work with those guys again?" he was quick to respond, "Now wait a minute, for whatever reason

Walt (left) *had always had a personal relationship with the members of his staff* (Joe Grant, middle; Jack Kinney, right), *but when the staff numbered more than one thousand, too many did not know him, or had never even been in a meeting with him.*

they did what they did, they thought they were right. We've had our differences on a lot of things, but we're going to continue making pictures, and we're going to find a way to work together."

For the supervising animators, making *Bambi* a quality film was not only our job, but our personal aspiration. It had been difficult to convince ourselves that this was still possible, and even more difficult to convince the other artists who would have to do it. The spark had gone out. But by November, we were starting to make progress, and once again we could believe that *Bambi* might finally be completed. After all, we had been through everything that year. What more could possibly happen?

The outstanding work of Ty Wong and others was evidence that making Bambi *a quality film was not only a job, but a personal aspiration of the artists and animators.*

On December 7, the Japanese bombed Pearl Harbor and we were at war. On the eighth, the Army took over the sound stage at the studio as a workshop for their trucks and storage for their equipment. Within days all future productions were shelved and everyone had new assignments on war-related projects, that is, everyone except those still on *Bambi.* Many weeks would be required to complete the last drawings, the ink and paint, the checking, the final camera, and all of the follow-up functions. We hoped we had that much time.

One last event—actually the lack of an event— did occur in 1941. A picture of our young elephant star, Dumbo, had been slated for the cover of *Time* magazine for the week of December 7. Such exposure would easily double the movie's attendance at Christmas time. Walt surely needed every nickel, but as with most everything else in 1941, he did not get what he had hoped for. The outbreak of the war was on the cover of every magazine in the country that week. *Dumbo* brought in a profit of $850,000, but we had expected twice that much. What was needed was four times that much! We could not face 1942 with much enthusiasm. It would be tough going the rest of the way.

A Masterpiece

I would hate to make another picture that would lose money.

—WALT DISNEY

The Japanese dominated the war in the Pacific all through those early months of 1942. Half of the studio's employees were drafted, enlisted, or left to take jobs in the defense industry. The enlarged Lockheed staff moved into the whole northern portion of the animation building, and our spirited cartoonists, recovering from their 1941 trauma, made drawings of huge wings being attached to the building. We were issued badges so we could be quickly identified by security officers who guarded every exit. In place of the small photo that appeared on each badge we drew faces of Pluto, Donald, deer, rabbits, and outlandish caricatures of ourselves. No one noticed!

The staff still working on *Bambi* felt completely deserted. All in all, probably no more than thirty-five or forty men and women were scurrying about, trying to finish the studio's final film from its Golden Age. There was not much excitement or the usual thrill of completion during the last days of *Bambi,* but finally it was finished.

A theater was chosen in Pomona, some forty miles east of Los Angeles, for our preview showing. On the evening of February 28, 1942, a small chartered bus took about fifteen of the studio's top personnel, directors, and supervisors to join the audience. Afterwards we would carry out any quick changes or cuts that might be needed. The ride to Pomona was quiet. Hushed voices dis-

Walt preferred to try things out, encouraging the experimentation that led to extraordinary artwork.

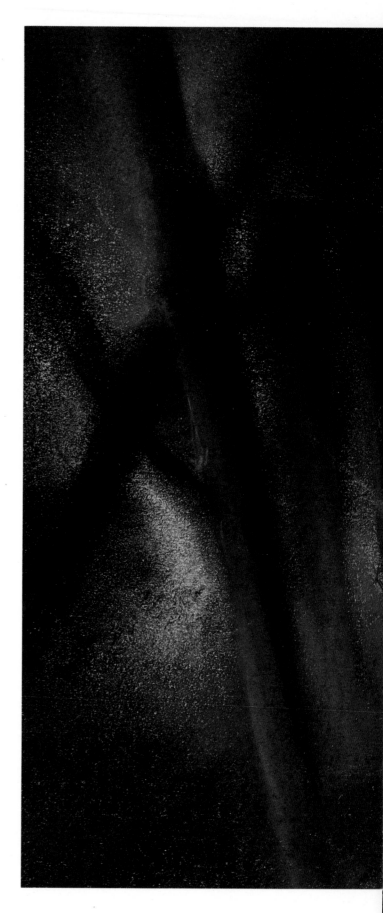

186

cussed everything except the film that had taken us seven years to complete. In the last screenings at the studio for employees and their friends, there had been mixed reactions. Some had said "beautiful" and "I loved those characters," while others sneered "too long" and "saccharine sweetness." We had corrected some of the sweetness, but how could the picture still be too long?

This film was certainly not what the theatergoers would expect from the Disney Studio, even after *Fantasia.* Our most recent release, *Dumbo,* had been what they wanted: bright, funny, fast moving, yet having a heart tug too. *Bambi* was not at all like that. None of us were sure it would even pay for itself. A large gross had never been our goal in the making of this sensitive portrayal of innocent animals trying to survive in surroundings both enchanting and threatening, but we did want people to come and see what we had done.

The theater was full of noisy, expectant patrons, a good house, people who wanted to be entertained. The opening went well; Thumper was an instant hit, and the audience even sat enraptured during the delightful April shower. The rigors of winter played to a very quiet house. Were they absorbed? Or merely patient? Even the shot that killed Bambi's mother brought little more than a slight gasp. But when Bambi returned through the big trees searching for her and crying, "Mother, where are you?" a teenage voice from up in the balcony answered derisively, "Here I am, Bambi!"

There was a momentary ripple of snickers, then silence again. That kind of response could have been just a brief release from tension, but we were crushed and angered and disappointed. The ride back to Burbank was even quieter than the ride out had been.

Walt dismissed the insensitive quip as unrepresentative of the audience and wisely would not consider making any changes in that part of the film. He concentrated instead on little bits and pieces that would play better with judicious editing. There were no retakes or new additions. The corrected, final version was released to the world on August 13, 1942.

The opening went well; the audience sat captivated through the April shower scene (above) *and Thumper, whose character had begun long ago in Mr. Hare* (below), *was an instant success.*

Parents were entranced with the wonderful characters of the forest creatures, but were unsure about the film's drama and violence.

It did not attract as many people as we had hoped, and the reviews were mixed. The critics were seeing something new from the studio and were unable to grasp its significance; their reviews were predominantly glib and breezy. Only years later did critics begin to sense the magnitude of the film's concept and the effect it would have on future viewers.

Most people who went to see *Bambi* were enthralled and deeply moved, but some parents thought it too disturbing for their children. Even though these parents were entranced with Thumper, Bambi, and Flower, they were not sure about the whole picture. Maybe it was too dramatic and violent in a world that was involved in a shattering war. *Bambi* did not recover its cost in this first release.

Walt wrote optimistically to Sidney Franklin in May of 1943 that their film was still "plugging along and it looks as though it will end up by paying its own way. When the war ends and the world markets are opened up, I know it will do well." It took longer than he had estimated, but when peace returned and the world was once more interested in beauty, fantasy, and magic, audiences discovered *Bambi*.

From the beginning, Sidney Franklin had envisioned in his mind just what he wanted *Bambi* to be. In contrast, Walt preferred to try things out, develop what looked good on the storyboards, and go with what was working. He had an approximate idea and offered many suggestions and possibilities, but he would never

All along, Walt knew that the characters of the forest animals would establish the entertainment Bambi *needed; Friend Owl* (top), *Flower* (middle), *Bambi and Faline* (bottom), *and Thumper* (right) *prove his point.*

Walt's approach to filmmaking fostered the subtle imagery and imagination that underscored this story of one deer from birth to maturity (above and opposite).

make everyone stick to a preconceived script. It sounds, perhaps, like a haphazard approach to filmmaking, but if his mind had been set at the start, he would not have discovered the value of Sidney Franklin's advice, or Marc Davis's drawings, or Ty Wong's exceptional backgrounds, or Peter Behn's voice, or the animation we were able to create, or the all-important music—all of which made the film so impressive.

Walt had hired talented people who would grow with him. While stimulating the members of his staff toward a certain type of material, he used what they offered, shaping it, adding to it, getting others to follow, until he had built the scattered ideas into a strong, cohesive film. Our version of *Bambi* could not have been made any other way. Even in the days of the greatest frustrations, his sense of proportion and value proved to be right for the picture and far beyond our own vision. One day in the early 1950s Walt came up to us

with a happy, relieved look on his face. He announced, "*Bambi* has just paid for itself!" From then on, year after year and generation after generation, it has continued to charm viewers, young and old, with its believable fantasy.

How could this different picture have survived through all the chaos, one disaster after another, of seven years of turmoil and uncertainties? One could almost believe it had taken on a life of its own which no misfortune could extinguish. As finally completed, *Bambi* is a film that leaves its mark. It is an experience. It goes beyond endearing characters, serious and violent incidents; it reaches the heart and lives there forever. It is truly a masterpiece. Of all the great pictures Walt Disney made, this was his favorite. It is ours, too.

THE ANIMATION

OLD STAG

RONNO
COMPARATIVE SIZES ONLY

BAMBI (Seq. 10.1 - 10.2
10.3 and 11.0)

BAMBI'S MOTHER

FALINE (Seq. 10.1 - 10.2
10.3 - 11.0)

Milt Kahl created the final designs for all the deer, which displayed the vitality and authority found in his sketches (above, below, and opposite); *Establishing exact comparative size was a necessary part of the development of all the characters* (opposite, bottom).

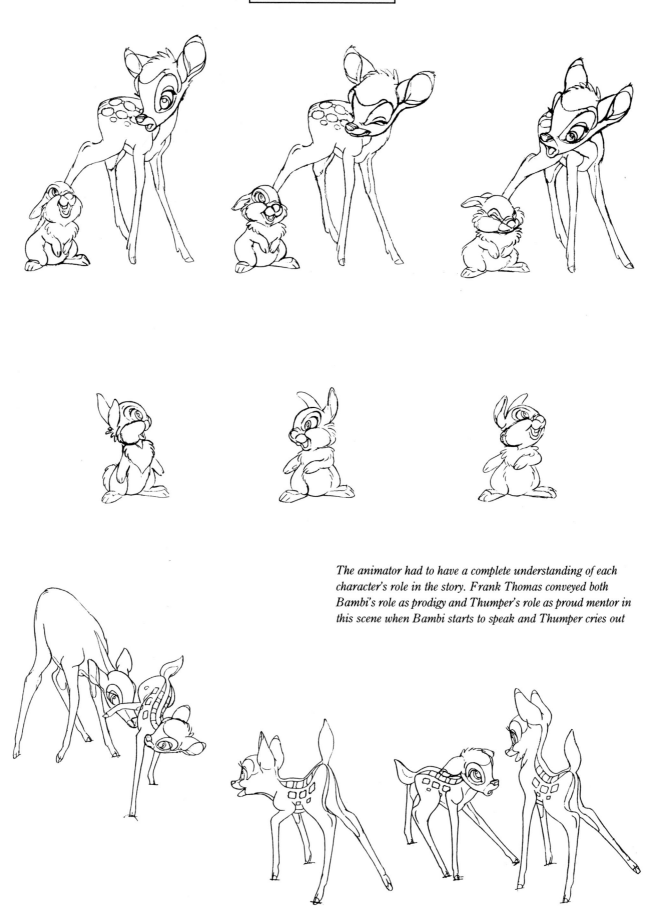

The animator had to have a complete understanding of each character's role in the story. Frank Thomas conveyed both Bambi's role as prodigy and Thumper's role as proud mentor in this scene when Bambi starts to speak and Thumper cries out

excitedly, "Look! He's trying to talk!" (top and above); When a shy Bambi does not want to say anything to the bold Faline, Frank Thomas's clarity of the characters' poses expresses their feelings in pantomime (below).

Eating greens is a special treat,
It makes long ears, and great big feet.
But it sure is awful stuff to eat!
I made that last part up myself.

Thumper had to show his disagreement that greens were better to eat than blossoms, not only in dialogue, but in acting, through Ollie Johnston's animation (below).

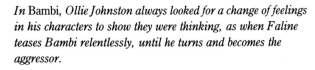

In Bambi, *Ollie Johnston always looked for a change of feelings in his characters to show they were thinking, as when Faline teases Bambi relentlessly, until he turns and becomes the aggressor.*

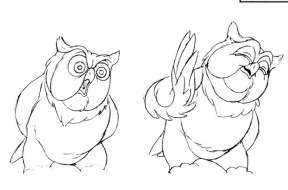

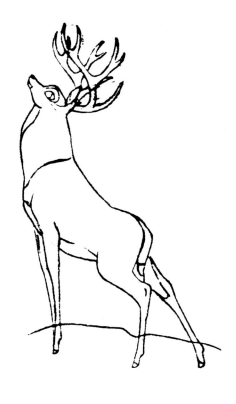

Together, Bernard Garbutt and Milt Kahl had the knowledge and understanding necessary to animate the large stag in exciting action, making him the strong, silent type rather than the wise philosopher (above and right).

Eric Larson used the owl's natural ability to spin its head in a dramatic combination of effects and personality (right). When animating the owl's dialogue, he relied on anthropomorphic gestures, actions and attitudes he remembered from people in his hometown (above).

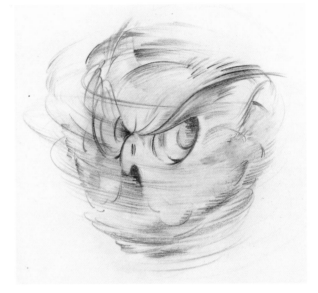

WALT DISNEY'S
BAMBI

From the Story by
FELIX SALTEN

Supervising Director
DAVID D. HAND

Story Direction
PERCE PEARCE

Story Adaptation
LARRY MOREY

Music by
FRANK CHURCHILL
EDWARD PLUMB

Orchestration by
CHARLES WOLCOTT
PAUL J. SMITH

Conducted by
ALEXANDER STEINERT

Choral Arrangements by
CHARLES HENDERSON

Story Development
GEORGE STALLINGS
MELVIN SHAW
CARL FALLBERG
CHUCK COUCH
RALPH WRIGHT

Sequence Directors
JAMES ALGAR
BILL ROBERTS
NORMAN WRIGHT
SAM ARMSTRONG
PAUL SATTERFIELD
GRAHAM HEID

Art Direction
THOMAS H. CODRICK

ROBERT C. CORMACK
McLAREN STEWART
DAVID HILBERMAN

AL ZINNEN
LLOYD HARTING
JOHN HUBLEY

DICK KELSEY

Backgrounds
MERLE T. COX

TYRUS WONG
ART RILEY
ROBERT McINTOSH
TRAVIS JOHNSON

W. RICHARD ANTHONY
STAN SPOHN
RAY HUFFINE
ED LEVITT

JOE STAHLEY

Supervising Animators
FRANKLIN THOMAS
MILTON KAHL
ERIC LARSON
OLIVER M. JOHNSTON, JR.

Animators

FRASER DAVIS
BILL JUSTICE
DON LUSK
RETTA SCOTT
KENNETH HULTGREN
KENNETH O'BRIEN
LOUIS SCHMITT

PRESTON BLAIR
JOHN BRADBURY
BERNARD GARBUTT
JOSHUA MEADOR
PHIL DUNCAN
GEORGE ROWLEY
ART PALMER

ART ELLIOTT

To
SIDNEY A. FRANKLIN
our sincere appreciation for his
inspiring collaboration

INDEX

ILLUSTRATION CREDITS

We have endeavored to accurately credit the artists responsible for the illustrations used throughout and offer our sincere apologies to any artist whose work has been mistakenly identified or unidentified.

Endpapers: Marc Davis; page 2: Harold Miles; page 3: Milt Kahl; pages 4-5: Robert McIntosh; page 7: Tyrus Wong; page 10: Tyrus Wong; page 12: Marc Davis; page 13: (middle) Fred Madison, (bottom) Louie Schmitt; pages 14-15: Tyrus Wong; page 16: (top) Fred Madison, (bottom) Lynn Karp; page 17: (bottom) Lynn Karp; page 18: (middle) Phil Duncan, (bottom) Ollie Johnston; page 19: (top) Tom Codrick, (middle) Murray McClelland, Harvey Toombs, Eric Larson, Supervisor; (bottom, left) Ollie Johnston, (bottom, right) Milt Kahl; page 20: Tyrus Wong; page 21: (top) Ken O'Brien, Fred Madison, Ollie Johnston, Supervisor, (middle) Ollie Johnston, Frank Thomas, (bottom, right) Ollie Johnston, Frank Thomas, (bottom, left) Louis Schmitt; page 22: (top to bottom) Milt Kahl; page 24: (middle) Milt Kahl, Frank Thomas, (bottom) Ollie Johnston; page 25: (top) Tyrus Wong, (bottom) Ollie Johnston; pages 26-27: Harold Miles; page 28: (top and middle) Frank Thomas, (bottom) Frank Thomas, Bambi; Harvey Toombs, birds; page 29: (top) Frank Thomas, (middle) Frank Thomas, Bambi; John McManus, butterfly; page 30: (top) Frank Thomas, Tom Palmer, Effects; page 31: (top) Marc Davis, (middle) Tyrus Wong, (bottom) Art Elliott; page 32 (top and bottom) Tyrus Wong; page 33: (clockwise from top left) Joseph Gayek, Cornett Wood; Ken Peterson, rabbits, Ugo D'Orsi, Effects; credit unknown; Murray McClelland, Joseph Gayek; credit unknown; Louie Schmitt; page 35: (top) Tyrus Wong; page 36: (top) Tyrus Wong; page 37: (top) Tyrus Wong; page 38 (top) Don Towsley; page 39: (top, left) Tyrus Wong, (middle) Ollie Johnston; page 40: (middle) Marc

Davis, (bottom) Frank Thomas; page 41: (bottom) Frank Thomas; page 42: (top) Tom Codrick, (middle) Paul Busch, (bottom) Ken Hultgren, Stag; Ollie Johnston, Bambi; page 43 (top) Bernard Garbutt, Dan Noonan, (middle) Bernard Garbutt, Louie Schmitt, John Sewall, (bottom) Murray McClelland, Eric Larson, Supervisor; page 44: (top) Ollie Johnston, (bottom) Ken Hultgren; page 45: (top) David Hall, (bottom) Ken Hultgren; page 46: (top and bottom) Ken Hultgren; page 47: (top and bottom) Don Lusk; page 50: (top) Bill Justice, (bottom, left and right) Phil Duncan, Frank Thomas, Supervisor; page 51: (top) Frank Thomas, (middle, right) Phil Duncan, (bottom) Phil Duncan, Frank Thomas, Supervisor; page 52: (top) Phil Duncan, (middle) Marc Davis; page 56: (top) Bill Justice, (middle) Bill Justice, George Rowley, Effects; (bottom) Art Elliott; page 58: (top) Bill Justice; page 59: (left) Bill Justice, (top, middle, and bottom, right) Milt Kahl; page 60: Tyrus Wong; page 62: (top) Murray McClelland, Eric Larson, Supervisor; (middle) Phil Duncan, George Rowley, Effects; (bottom) Marc Davis, John McManus, Effects; page 63: (top) Paul Busch, Fred Madison, (bottom) Fred Madison; page 66: (top, left and right) Phil Duncan, Milt Kahl, Supervisor; page 67: (top) Phil Duncan, Milt Kahl, Supervisor; (bottom) Phil Duncan, Milt Kahl, Supervisor; George Rowley, Effects; page 69: (bottom) Milt Kahl; page 71: (middle) Jack Bradbury; pages 72-73: (top and bottom) Jack Bradbury, Milt Kahl, Supervisor; page 74: (bottom) Jack Bradbury, Milt Kahl, Supervisor; page 75: (clockwise from top) Jack Bradbury, Milt Kahl, Supervisor; (middle) Preston Blair, George Rowley, Effects; page 78: Special Effects Department; page 79: (top and middle) Milt Kahl; page 80: (top) Milt Kahl, John McManus, Effects; page 81: (middle, left and right) Don Lusk, (bottom) Frank Grundeen, J. S. Escalante; page 84: (top) Retta Scott; page 85: Retta Scott; page 86: Retta Scott; page 87: Retta Scott, Milt Kahl; page 88: (top) John Sewall, Milt Kahl, Supervisor; (bottom, left) Retta Scott, (bottom, right) Retta Scott, dogs; Jack Bradbury, deer; page 89: (top, left and right) John Sewall, Milt Kahl, Supervisor; (middle and bottom) Don Lusk, Milt Kahl, Supervisor; page 90: (top) John McManus, (middle) John McManus, Ken Peterson; page 91: (top) Tyrus Wong, (middle and bottom) Don Lusk, Milt Kahl, Supervisor; pages 92-93: Tyrus Wong; page 94: (bottom) John Sewall, John Reed, Art Palmer, John Noel Tucker, Effects; page 95: (from top to bottom) Bernard Garbutt, John Reed, Art Palmer, Effects; Ken Hultgren; Ken Hultgren, Art Palmer, Effects; Ken Hultgen; page 96: Tom Codrick; page 97: (bottom) Phil Duncan, Milt Kahl, Supervisor; page 100: (middle) Dan Noonan, (bottom) Ollie Johnston, John McManus, Effects; page 101: (top) Ken Hultgren, (bottom) Ollie Johnston, Ken O'Brien; page 102: Gustaf Tenggren; page 113: Marc Davis; page 116: Milt Kahl, Retta Scott; page 117: (middle and bottom) Retta Scott; page 120: (top and bottom) Ken Hultgren; page 121: (top and bottom) Tyrus Wong; pages 122-23: Tyrus Wong; page 127: (right) Murray McClelland, Eric Larson, Supervisor; page 134: Tyrus Wong; page 135: Tom Codrick; page 139: (bottom) Milt Kahl; page 142: (bottom) Frank Thomas, Milt Kahl; page 149: Frank Thomas, Milt Kahl; page 150: (top) Eric Larson; page 161: (top) Lynn Karp, (bottom, left) Frank Thomas; page 162: (top) Milt Kahl; page 163: Tom Codrick; page 169: (bottom) Retta Scott, Milt Kahl; page 173: (top and bottom) Art Elliott; page 175: Milt Kahl; page 178: (bottom) Lew Keller; page 182: Tyrus Wong; pages 186-87: Tyrus Wong; page 188: (top) Josh Meador, J. Will, (bottom) Tom Codrick; page 189: Tom Codrick; page 190: (top) Marc Davis, (middle) Bill Justice, (bottom) Milt Kahl; page 193: Tyrus Wong.

Designed by J. C. Suarès and Paul Zakris

Set in Century Old Style by
Graphic Arts Composition
Philadelphia, Pennsylvania

Printed and bound by
Toppan Printing Company, Ltd.,
Tokyo, Japan